○ Collins need t

Weddings

D0441385

Collins **need to know?**

Weddings

All the information, advice and inspiration
you need for the perfect wedding

Cathy Howes

First published in 2005 by
Collins, an imprint of
HarperCollins*Publishers*
77-85 Fulham Palace Road
Hammersmith, London W6 8JB

The Collins website address is:
www.collins.co.uk

08 07
5 4 3 2

A catalogue record for this book is available from the British Library

Created by: Essential Works
Project Editor: Mani Ramaswamy
Designer: Kate Ward
Cover design: Cook Design
Front cover photograph: Getty Images/Victoria Pearson
Back cover photographs: Kerry Morgan (www.rethinkweddings.com)

ISBN-13 978 0 00 719703 3
ISBN-10 0 00 719703 9

Colour reproduction by Colourscan, Singapore
Printed and bound by Printing Express Ltd, Hong Kong

contents

Doing it your way

The minute you announce your engagement you'll be offered advice – from the older generation in your family, to people you hardly know. Most of it will be well-meant, but much of it won't suit you. Never forget, your wedding is all about you and should be an enjoyable transition from two happy singles to one happy couple, not an endurance test!

Marriage is an institution and however determined you are to resist tradition, weddings are steeped in it. Behind the desire to be modern and different, there is often a little girl teetering about in her mum's high heels with a net curtain on her head. Most girls dream of their wedding day long before they meet the man who will take the starring role, and the secret to a successful wedding, especially with so much choice today, is to use customs and traditions as a template and stamp some kind of individuality on the day.

Ever-changing world

Since the Marriage Act of 1994 and the growth of approved licensed premises in the UK, the civil ceremony has taken on a new lease of life. Prior to 1994, couples who did not feel at home in a religious setting, or who were divorced and unable to remarry in church, were restricted to ceremonies in a register office. These were usually quick to arrange and simple in structure but often low-key and unfussy due to a lack of space and time. With the change in the law, however, many venues began applying for a wedding licence, and now there are so many different settings – from hotels, museums and castles to sports stadia, zoos and race courses – that civil ceremonies now outnumber traditional church services. (In London, for instance, only around 20 per cent of weddings are in churches.)

However, if you don't choose a religious ceremony, this doesn't mean that everything associated with this style will be thrown out of the window. Apart from the obvious missing elements of a spiritual service – hymns, religious readings, organ music and a minister of religion – many of the new-style civil celebrations are shaped using the traditional framework but embellished with personal and unique touches for each couple. Writing your own vows has become increasingly popular and although certain denominations allow only the minimum tinkering, many ministers and registrars are happy to work with a couple to personalize their vows. In the increasingly popular Humanist ceremonies, for instance, couples often write their own script, although these are not legally recognized ceremonies and couples have to be legally married in a civil ceremony beforehand.

With *Collins need to know? Weddings* we outline the essentials, suggest alternative styles of wedding, touch on traditions and suggest how these customary elements can be used as a framework for a truly individual modern wedding. We hope to inform, inspire and reassure. Where advice is given with emphasis, it is largely based on prior experience.

Getting

prepared

As well as the ongoing plans for 'the big day', there are all those plans for 'the big life together' to consider, too. The practicalities of living together, agreeing household budgets and building a home for the future are just as important – if not more so – as deciding on the colours for the bridesmaids' sashes and choosing the readings.

Living together

Choosing to share a home with another person is a big step. For some couples, it is an even bigger step than getting married itself, which, after they have decided to share an address, a bed and all the financial obligations that cohabitating entails, they see as the cherry on the cake. The truth is that both decisions are life-changing ones.

'You never really know someone until you live with them...' is a phrase you hear often, and from different perspectives – through the gritted teeth of someone who has recently split up with a live-in lover, or as part of the contented musings of a couple celebrating their silver wedding anniversary. But it is true, and moving in together is often the true test of a relationship.

Are you moving in with him, is he moving in with you or will you be choosing a new, neutral address in which to start your life together? Bear in mind that some small resentments are natural, particularly if the person being 'descended upon' has lived independently for a while. Things are kept in a certain place, done in a certain way and the sudden loss of space – storage and otherwise – can give rise to tensions.

MUST KNOW

Money matters

- Quite apart from discovering your partner likes to pick his toenails in the kitchen, one of the biggest wake-up calls can be discovering your loved-one's attitude to finance.
- When you decide to live together, openness about money is paramount and any attempts to keep things secret from each other is not a healthy start.
- Obviously you both need to retain some financial independence, but establish early on which bills and costs are to be shared and set up direct debits or standing orders, or a joint account, to take care of this (see page 20).
- Couples row about money more than any other issue – ask any relationship counsellor or divorce lawyer.

▶ Living together is the outward, tangible sign that tells the rest of the world you are a couple. Getting married – for all its public display of affection and the traditional symbols of cake and confetti – is the personal and private commitment that seals a relationship.

Rose-coloured spectacles

The most successful relationships are built on love and trust. Behind all the fantasy film scripts and glitzy advertisements featuring 'successful' couples is a lot of artistic licence. Driving all the glossy magazine shots of celebrity couples smiling from perfect bijou apartments are a lot of make-up artists and home stylists plus two individuals who probably bicker and sulk just like any other couple.

If you love someone enough to want to share an address with them, you are going to have to learn to live with all the annoying or irritating little foibles and habits that make up that person. Encouraging someone to pick up wet towels or put the cap back on the toothpaste is one thing, but trying to fundamentally change someone can be damaging to a relationship. Presumably you decided to live together so that you could evolve as a couple. Any therapist will tell you that 'evolve' is the healthier interpretation of 'change'.

MUST KNOW

Couples that realize compromise is sometimes necessary and try to take account of the other's feelings are going to fare much better than those who start measuring each other's space. On the other hand, moving in together is also a good time to let go of a bit of the past and move on. Ask yourself if you really need to keep all those clothes/vinyl albums/football programmes/old copies of *Vogue*?

What is a wedding?

A wedding is not just a 'day', although that's how it can seem when the future hinges on one particular date. A wedding is a point in time when a couple says 'ok, what we have together is so real, we've decided to commit the rest of our lives to each other'.

In previous generations, a wedding was a precursor to starting a family and buying a home, so it was a rite of passage that many couples took without much thought. Today, the stigma that once ostracized a couple who lived together, or had a child outside of wedlock, has all but gone and some couples often marry long after the ink is dry on the mortgage papers and the patter of tiny feet can be heard. The social pressure to get married has relaxed, which means couples who take the plunge today are likely to be doing it because the time and the person are right.

Let's go round again

As much as a book like this would like to trumpet the fact that marriage is forever, in many cases it is not. The divorce rate in the UK is around one in three – some figures put it as high as one in nearly two. According to the National Stepfamily Association, one in eight children lives with a step family and it has predicted that by the year 2010, most people will cohabit, marry, divorce and then remarry. Yet a poll in 2001 showed that three-quarters of the British population still believe in marriage.

Time to talk

Obviously there is no official time a couple should spend together before they begin to talk about marriage. Some of the most enduring marriages are born from whirlwind romances. On the other hand, most people know of a couple that lived happily together for ten years, got married and split up less than a year later. The secret, as any relationship counsellor will

MUST KNOW

Legalities

● There is no legal requirement for a married woman to change her surname or for children to take one or other of their parents' surnames.

● Your spouse automatically becomes your next of kin and marriage will usually supersede any previous wills.

● With the abolition of the married couple's allowance, tax-wise there are no particular financial advantages to being married.

confirm, is communication. It is rare that a couple will agree on everything and mirror each other on every level, but if they communicate properly, at least they will be able to recognize and address their differences and spot any potential difficulty before it becomes a hurdle.

Relate to each other

Relate is a national registered charity in the UK with over 50 years' experience of helping people with their relationships. It offers counselling services and marriage-preparation courses, which are open to everyone considering either a religious or secular service. Relate's aim is to improve communication and understanding and to avoid conflict.

◄ Now that marriage is often more of a lifestyle choice than a natural or inevitable progression, many couples choose to get married at the same time as their child or children are baptized or have a naming ceremony.

Who gets married?

The cynical might say 'the incurably romantic' but today's couples are more mature and more independent than their predecessors. They are also far more innovative and daring.

Brides and grooms are getting older, or rather they are choosing to marry later, and this, coupled with financial independence, has influenced who controls the preparations. In the early 1990s, a couple getting married were in their mid-20s (25 for the bride, 26 for the groom). Since 1999, however, the average age of a British man getting married for the first time has risen to above 30 and his bride is likely to be 28, although she, too, looks set to tip over the 30 mark by the end of this decade. In the past, a couple would marry in their parish church, the bride's father would pay for a modest wedding breakfast, friends would give handy gifts like frying pans and the couple would move in together for the first time after the big day.

◀ Today, in all likelihood, the engaged couple is already living together with considerable financial independence, have more than enough frying pans and an income which means they can pay for – and dictate – the style of their own wedding.

What will it cost?

- Surveys showing the average cost of a wedding vary according to who has commissioned the poll and what they are trying to prove, but it is fair to say that in 2004, £15,000 was not an unusual total figure.
- One survey by an internet bank worked out that if you tot up the entire cost of a UK wedding in the 21st century, including guests' accommodation, presents and transport, the day costs £61 per minute – that's £1 a second.
- A broadsheet newspaper study in 2003 estimated that in order to celebrate your big day with you, the average cost to each guest can be as much as £500 if you take into account the hen/stag night, accommodation, travel, gift and outfit. The average cost of a female guest's outfit was around £175, and the average spend per person on a gift was in the region of £50. Bearing in mind just how much your nearest and dearest will ultimately spend, the pressure to give them a day to remember just goes on increasing.

Can you really do that?

However unique your ceremony, every wedding has to follow certain legal structures and use statutory wording, but the freedom to cock a snook at tradition and do something 21st century on top of the legal basics is there if you want it. In recent years marriages have been broadcast live on the internet and one couple recited their vows at Birkenhead Town Hall before the registrar and, at the same time, into mobile phones so that relatives 3,000 miles away in Philadelphia could take part. The church hall and social club are no longer the obvious venues for receptions. One British couple celebrated their ceremony at Stockport Register Office with a feast at a fast food restaurant and HRH the Queen has even opened Balmoral Castle for certain members of staff to celebrate their nuptials.

Same-sex weddings

A survey in 2004 revealed that over 1000 gay couples in the UK have tied the knot in partnership ceremonies since they were introduced shortly after the new millennium. Although gay couples have not enjoyed the same recognition as heterosexual couples, the Civil Partnership Bill, which is set to become law by late 2005, will give same-sex couples the chance to take part in a civil ceremony and accord them the same rights as married couples. No religious content will be allowed and there will be a dissolution process similar to divorce. As the law stands in 2004, only Holland, Belgium, and certain parts of the USA and Canada recognize same-sex marriage.

Buying a home

Living as a couple means not only that you are sensitive to your partner's happiness, but that you are both responsible for your combined finances and the roof over your heads. To live in harmony, you need to take some practical early steps.

First-time buyers

If it is your first property you'll be able to share the joys (and perils) of house-hunting together. Before you set foot in an estate agent's, work out how much deposit you can rake together and how much you could realistically borrow on a mortgage. Any building society or bank will talk you through the qualifications for a mortgage, i.e. how many multiples of individual or joint salaries they use as their criteria. Many estate agents also have advisors who will offer to find you a good deal, but be sure they are not tied to one lender. Some may use a panel of five or six lenders, for example, which may not be enough choice to give you the best offer.

Being a first-time buyer puts you in a good bargaining position. You have nothing to sell and therefore form a less complicated chain, although if you are in rented accommodation you will have to give notice. Use this unfettered status to your advantage when trying to negotiate the asking price. Most agents and vendors will ask if your mortgage is already in place, so it is an idea to get an agreement in principle. The mortgage world is bewildering so whatever you do, seek advice and lots of it. Ask friends what they borrowed, how, and from whom. Remember they have your best interests at heart. A broker or sales person gets a commission.

TOP TIP

Anyone buying a property in the UK is liable for Stamp Duty on completion. The rates of Stamp Duty (as at 2004) are:
- Property up to £60,000 – NIL
- £60,001 TO £250.000 – 1%
- £250,001 TO £500,000 – 3%
- Over £500,000 – 4%

So if you can only just scrape together a deposit, bear in mind that a house costing £150,000 will cost you an extra £1,500 in Stamp Duty.

BEFORE YOU BUY A HOUSE YOU MUST BUDGET FOR:

- Deposit
- Solicitor's fees
- Local authority searches
- Property survey
- Stamp Duty
- Mortgage signing-on fee*
- Removal costs

* If applicable

If you are buying only, you are not liable for the estate agent's fees, which are the responsibility of the vendor.

What happens?

When you have made an offer on a property and it has been accepted, you will be sent a memorandum of sale and may have to lodge the deposit with your solicitor. A series of letters will then fly back and forth about things such as fixtures and fittings and local authority searches until both or all parties are in a position to exchange contracts. Up until this point, your vendor may pull out at any time, without explanation, even though you have spent money on surveys, solicitors and searches. This is the (often criticized) law in the UK and Wales; in Scotland, the law is more protective of the buyer. In all things, therefore, the mantra should be, take legal advice. After exchange of contracts there are usually two weeks until completion. It can be less, even the next day in some circumstances, but solicitors prefer at least one working week to get the paperwork straight. The completion date is the day when all monies are received from mortgage lenders and the day you can actually take possession of the property. From this point on you are liable, so make sure all contents and buildings insurance policies are in place.

MUST KNOW

Get a solicitor who specializes in conveyancing. Don't attempt to do it all yourself unless you have a shrewd understanding of property law and a lot of patience.

Joint finances

Whether you are renting from a local authority, a housing association or a private landlord, both names should be on the rental agreement. If one of you is moving into premises previously inhabited by the other, it is as well to change the rental agreement to cover both. This is not only a symbolic gesture of trust and sharing, it also means – should it all end in tears – that you both have equal redress and rights over the property.

Adequate cover

The same could be said about life cover on a mortgaged property. Since a home is the biggest financial commitment anyone is likely to make, ensure that you are adequately covered should one partner die. Cohabiting couples do not have the same automatic rights as married couples, and while you may be justified in arguing your case, it may be harder to prove without a valid will, particularly if your partner has been married before and has dependents. Treat the moving-in-together step as the big one as far as finances are concerned and have everything legally covered, including a will.

What about pre-nuptial agreements?

These are controversial and have their critics. A trend which has its roots in America, pre-nups were traditionally favoured by the stars who stood to lose a great deal in the law courts if their marriages failed. Today they are designed to ring-fence property or assets that an individual held before becoming part of a couple. They tend to ease the transition back to singlehood if things go wrong but are not definitive and can be contested in the courts.

MUST KNOW

If one of you earns significantly more than the other, or one of you is not working, it makes financial sense for investments or savings to be in the name of the low- or non-earner.

Taxing issues

Being married no longer carries automatic tax benefits and you will both be taxed individually, although if one or both of you was previously a lone parent, your marriage may affect the amount of Child Benefit you receive and will change your entitlement to, or amount of, Child Tax Credit. Inform both departments of the Inland Revenue as soon as you are able to following the wedding.

A change from lone parent status or a move from lone to joint occupancy will also negate the status discount you may have been receiving in respect of council tax from your local authority, so be sure to inform them in writing.

Clean up

Creating a joint 'living fund' often provides a good opportunity to overhaul all your finances, including your credit and store cards. If you discover that the combined plastic between you is a bit drastic, take a good look at your monthly credit card and store card statements and work out which of the card companies are offering the most competitive interest rates.

It may be that once you live together and bills are reduced or halved, the need for one or both of you to use credit cards at all will soon be reduced anyway. Perhaps it would be easier to add an additional cardholder name to an existing card with a low- or interest-free deal and cut up the others? Remember that many companies offer worthwhile introductory fixed-term, no-interest offers for transfer balances. Whatever you do, make sure you both have adequate home insurance to cover loss of any cards.

MUST KNOW

Living together and getting married is a time to be open about all the savings schemes, forgotten shares or premium bonds you may hold. Often, little things can add up to a lot. If one of you has been paying into a low-performing endowment, for instance, to pay off a mortgage, once you get your joint mortgage (and the original single loan it was taken out to cover is no longer active), it may be more economic to cash in/auction off the endowment and reinvest the money into a joint savings account or ISA, or use it to boost a pension fund. Before doing anything, seek the advice, together, of an independent financial adviser (IFA).

Shared expenses

There is an old saying that two people can live as cheaply as one and in some instances there is a great deal of truth in that. To get a good idea of how much living together is going to cost (or save) you, simply fill in the amounts that you know in the chart below and estimate the remainder. Remember that some utility providers offer discounts to customers who make their payments by monthly direct debit.

Joint finances planning chart

FIXED COSTS	Per month	Per quarter	Per year
Mortgage/rent.			
Council tax			
Buildings insurance.			
Contents insurance.			
Service charges (for flats)			
Life assurance			
(and/or critical illness cover) . . .			
Private healthcare.			
Water charges.			
Electricity bill.			
Gas bill			
Television licence			
Telephone bill (rental and calls) .			
Internet service provider			
Cable/additional TV services. . .			
Car/s road tax.			
Car/s insurance.			
TOTAL			

VARIABLE COSTS	Weekly estimates	Monthly estimates
Grocery shopping		
Commuting costs		
Petrol		
Entertaining and socializing. . . .		
TOTAL		

▲ Getting married means cooperating over all areas of your life together, particularly your finances. Try to avoid being judgemental about each other's spending habits. One of you may clean the car by hand, the other may pay for a car wash. So what? It's not worth falling out over a few pounds.

Nothing too small

In the excitement of moving in together it is easy to overlook small things that could add up and start costing you money. Go through your bank statement and cancel any direct debits which were active on your old property.

Make sure credit card companies know you have moved and have your post redirected for a few months. You don't want to be hit with late-payment charges because you forgot to tell them your new address. If one you is self-employed, keep all documents relating to things like phone line rental, call charges or internet connection charges as these may be tax deductible.

want to know more?

Take it to the next level...

Go to...
▶ **Living together** – page 10
▶ **Shared expenses** – page 20
▶ **Now you are married** – page 176

Other sources
▶ **www.fsa.gov.uk**
The Financial Services Authority offers online guidance on finding an IFA, or call their consumer helpline on 0845 606 1234 for more information
▶ **www.inlandrevenue.gov.uk**
Child Benefit and Child Tax Credit are both administered by the Inland Revenue

Getting

engaged

There's no bigger giveaway to a forthcoming wedding than a recently engaged woman constantly playing with her newly acquired ring. Yet getting engaged is about so much more than jewellery. It's about sharing the good news, marking the occasion and trying to contain your growing excitement while you plan your future together.

Getting engaged

Congratulations, he's asked you to marry him. Or maybe you asked him? Either way, you've finally mentioned the 'm' word. Whether the proposal was made to romantic violin music or was a casual remark at the supermarket checkout, life will never be the same again...

Engagements have come a long way since the days when a groom looked around for a prospective bride, settled on his victim and simply kidnapped her. Saxon King Ethelbert tried to put a stop to this rather 'basic' courtship ritual by making engagements a legal requirement for marriage, and even as recently as Victorian times, an engagement was legally binding. Once a suitor had formally asked a woman's father for permission to marry, the couple was betrothed and the bride-to-be's family could sue the bounder if he broke his promise.

Today an engagement is not binding in the eyes of the law, but more of a public display of commitment, a suitable planning period for the big day and a great excuse for a party and some jewellery shopping. There is no set period for an engagement – it is generally as long as it needs to be for the couple to save up for and plan the wedding of their dreams.

◀ As a general rule when wording engagement announcements and invitations, 'son/daughter of' is taken to mean the only son or daughter; 'younger/elder' implies there are two sons or daughters; and 'youngest/eldest' means there are at least three brothers and sisters.

Spreading the news

Traditionally the groom formally asked the bride's father for permission to marry his daughter. Today, most independent brides would find that an antiquated approach although many grooms still like to have that little man-to-man chat anyway, as a courtesy. Either way, telling close family about your wedding plans is one of the most exciting stages in a relationship and, alas, the first potential upset if you are not fortunate enough to be able to announce your news at a big family occasion.

If you decide to tell the bride's family first, fill the groom's family in on the news very soon afterwards, especially if the two sides have acquaintances in common. A peeved mother-of-the-groom can spend many months brooding over being a long way down the list of who was told when! News of a wedding usually spreads organically, especially in the era of e-mail and text messaging, so making a formal newspaper announcement can seem quaint. However, if one or both sets of parents are keen to announce the engagement to the world and you have no objection, it is a nice gesture to let the older generation enjoy the moment. If you want to stick to customs, the bride's parents traditionally paid for any announcements in the national press and the groom's covered anything which appeared in regional papers.

WORDING YOUR ANNOUNCEMENT

In terms of wording, it is increasingly common for the couple to enter their own, fairly simple statement such as:
Cathy Cook and Ray Rogers
Cathy and Ray, together with their friends and family, are pleased to announce their engagement...

Another format is for the announcement to come from one set of parents, particularly if this is in a local newspaper:
Mr and Mrs James Cook are pleased to announce the engagement of their daughter Cathy to [Mr] Ray Rogers, elder son of Mr and Mrs David Rogers of Bexley, Kent.

For a national announcement, both families need to be geographically placed, so the following wording may be helpful:
The engagement is announced between Ray Rogers, elder son of Mr and Mrs David Rogers of Bexley Kent, and Cathy Cook, youngest daughter of Mr and Mrs James Cook of Plymouth, Devon.

MUST KNOW

Special wording for divorced or widowed parents.
These examples refer to the bride's family, but the principles could equally apply to the groom's. They are also useful guidelines when wording invitations (see Chapter 5). Who is mentioned and who is left off is a delicate point. Relatively new step-parents do not necessarily need to be named, nor do long-estranged birth parents. The father/step-father, mother/step-mother whose name appears is generally the one to whom the bride or groom is closest and who is viewed in the parental role.
● If the bride's mother has divorced and remarried: *Cathy, youngest daughter of Mrs Deborah Dyke and Mr James Cox...*
● If the bride's mother is widowed: *Cathy, youngest daughter of Mrs Deborah Cox and the late Mr James Cox...*
● If the bride's mother was widowed and remarried to someone who has figured prominently in the bride's life: *Cathy, youngest daughter of the late Mr James Cox and Mrs Deborah Dyke and step-daughter to Mr Donald Dyke...*

Engagement photos

Royals and celebrities often commission an engagement photo, so why not you? It may not appear on the front page of a glossy magazine, but it could be used alongside any newspaper announcements, and it is a great way to illustrate your news when e-mailing old friends and contacts. Obviously a sitting at a studio is something you may not have factored into the budget, but it is a good way to try out a professional you may be considering for the wedding album and in this light, it is money well spent. Better still, ask if it would be possible for your photographer to take the shot at a reception venue you are considering and try everything out at once!

Presents

Some people may want to give you a gift to mark your engagement. This can be tricky if you have barely thought about what you want to do about a wedding gift list, let alone an engagement one. If friends are insistent, suggest they take you out for a celebratory drink or meal which you can all enjoy. If the persistent request comes from the older generation, such as a great aunt or a grandparent, it is good manners to think of something, even if it is just a frame for a favourite photo, as these relatives come from a generation that did things 'properly' and that includes giving loved ones engagement presents. Suffice to say, if the wedding is called off, engagement presents should be returned.

Time to party?

Everyone immediately expects a 'do' when an engagement is announced, but if the wedding is only a few months away, you may feel it will:

- take the shine off the biggest party of all at the reception.
- make guests feel obliged to buy you a present twice.
- eat horribly into your budget.
- pre-determine who will be on your wedding guest list. When trying to keep the numbers down later, you may feel obliged to include everyone invited to your engagement party.

Getting to know you

To get around the pressure to throw a party, you could arrange a small family supper/meal out instead, which is a good opportunity for both sets of parents to meet, if they haven't yet, or get to know each other better. However, take care to avoid the 'm' word – that's money, not marriage. Many people can get embarrassed about finances so ask both sets of parents to stay off the subject of who is paying for what at the wedding during the initial meeting.

▼ If you feel brave enough you could book a meal in a restaurant for your two sets of parents, minus you and your fiancé. That way they can relax and get to know each other without feeling they have to be on their best behaviour.

Choosing a ring

Apart from the broad grins across your faces, the one big visual clue to your newly engaged state is the ring. Although suitors in films like to pop the question with a rock the size of a duck's egg, in the real world most brides prefer a say in the ring they will be wearing for the rest of their lives.

Custom dictates that a man should spend one month's salary on an engagement ring. Although no-one is too sure where that superstition originates (goldsmiths or diamond dealers presumably?), that's one tradition the bride may be keener to follow than the groom. However, it underlines what a careful decision-making process this has to be. The good news is that while choosing an engagement ring, a couple can also look around at possible wedding bands to complement the first ring and get a feel for metals, styles and prices, although it has always been considered unlucky to actually buy them at the same time.

◄ When choosing a style of engagement ring, bear in mind the type of work you do and whether you need to be careful of it catching. A raised setting is not ideal for a nurse, teacher or other 'hands-on' professional. A bezel setting, where the gem is surrounded and secured by the band, may be better.

Diamonds are forever

The most usual stone for an engagement ring is a diamond, traditionally representing lasting love. The ancient Greek and Latin names for diamonds mean 'unconquerable' and they are certainly one of the hardest minerals on earth. When choosing a diamond, the price will give you the most obvious clue to its quality, but it is also worth remembering the four factors that the professionals use to judge a diamond, known as the four Cs.

● **Cut** This is what gives the diamond its sparkle. Each flat surface cut into the gem is known as a facet. The better these surfaces can direct light into the diamond, the better the light is reflected back, making the gem more dazzling. Jewellers also refer to a diamond's fire, which is the stone's ability to reflect the colours of a rainbow. The way a diamond is cut adds to its value just as much as its weight (carat).

● **Clarity** Virtually all diamonds have slight impurities or inclusions. These are traces of gases or minerals trapped within the stone which can look like feathers or minuscule crystals and are usually only visible to a jeweller with a magnifying glass. Fewer than one per cent of diamonds are completely flawless.

● **Carat** The weight of a diamond is measured in carats (not to be confused with the carat measuring system in gold). There are 100 points in a carat and you are likely to see diamonds described in measurements such as 0.25 of a carat. Diamonds of more than 1 carat are very valuable and quite rare.

● **Colour** Most diamonds are colourless, although their slight yellow or brown tones come from trace elements in the stone. They are rated on a scale from D, meaning completely colourless, to Z, which is the deepest colour.

Other little gems

Modern brides are increasingly moving away from traditional diamond rings, going instead for a variety of colours and styles, not least because you can often get more semi-precious stone for your money. Alternatively, a larger coloured stone, set centrally and surrounded by tiny diamonds, combines the best of both worlds. Birthstones are often a good guide, each offering its own rich colour and individual meaning, but don't think you can choose only from your own birth date. Choose for message as well as month.

MONTH	COLOURED STONE	MEANING
January	Garnet (deep red to orange or yellowy brown)	Faithfulness and truth
February	Amethyst (rich violet purple)	Sincerity
March	Aquamarine (pale blue to light blue green)	Courage and hope
April	Diamond (usually colourless)	Joy and innocence
May	Emerald (leafy emerald green)	Hope and success
June	Pearl (usually white with hints of other colours)	Purity
July	Ruby (vermilion to violet red)	Emotional contentment
August	Peridot (transparent olive green)	Inspiration and understanding
September	Sapphire (usually clear blue)	Emotional balance and wisdom
October	Opal (white, grey or black with iridescent flecks)	Loveableness
November	Topaz (yellow, honey-coloured, golden brown or brown-blue)	Faithfulness and joy
December	Turquoise (rich blue, pale sky blue, green-blue or pale green)	Domestic harmony and prosperity

Styles and settings

- Popular settings include a prong or rivet setting (where the stone is held in small claws), a cluster (where small stones surround a larger one), a bezel setting (where a ring of metal holds the stone), a bar setting (where each stone is held by vertical metal bars) and a pavé or invisible setting (where almost no metal is visible between the stones). Someone with a more manual job may find a bezel setting less vulnerable than a high-pronged one.

- Diamonds are usually set in 9, 18 or 22 carat gold or platinum. The purest gold is 24 carat but this is too soft for most jewellery. Platinum is the most hard-wearing. Yellow gold is generally the most popular, although rose, red or white gold (usually more expensive) is a good talking point, even though these can lose a little brilliance. Whatever you choose, the same weight of gold should be used for your wedding band, otherwise you will always have a more durable metal wearing away a more vulnerable one.

- A well-fitting ring should be able to twist easily but need a little persuasion coming over the knuckle. When trying sizes, remember fingers shrink in cold weather and swell in heat. If you are not sure, err on the big side; you can always have a little metal removed. It's not so easy the other way around.

Where to look

High street jewellers are good for getting ideas, but you may want to search a little further afield or commission a ring of your own. As with most things, shop around, and ask any friends who have had jewellery made. Some jewellery designers specialize in band work and metal effects but commission someone else to set the stone. Check how many stages will be involved and any hidden costs. If you are considering an antique ring, buy from a reputable trader and make sure you can get it independently valued for insurance purposes.

Family heirlooms

There may be pressure to wear a ring belonging to a mother or grandmother. If you really don't want to but need to keep the peace, consider if the stone could be removed and made into another piece of jewellery such as a necklace.

want to know **more?**

Take it to the next level...

Go to...
► Choosing a photographer – page 82
► Invitation wording – page 88
► Gift lists – page 90

Other sources
► British Jewellers' Association members www.bja.org.uk
► Websites
 www.diamondgeezer.com
 www.icecool.co.uk
 www.adiamondisforever.com
 www.thediamondbuyingguide.com
► Engagement and Wedding Rings, Antoinette L Matlins and Antonio C Bonanno, from www.amazon.co.uk

The

legalities

While some elements of your wedding will leave you bewildered by choice, there are other considerations that are fixed and constant. Your registrar or religious minister will talk you through all the legal niceties, but it is worth being aware of all the documents you may need and the notice you must give, in plenty of time.

Keep it legal

A wedding is not only a joyous and public celebration of love, it's also a legally binding agreement, so be sure to find out (and fully understand) the legal requirements laid down for your chosen ceremony before you post the invitations.

Getting married in the UK

There are certain fundamental rules common to all ceremonies, civil or religious, in the UK. No matter how flamboyant or breathtaking the plans for your ceremony, you have to dot every 'i' and cross every 't' if you want it to be legal. Naturally the jargon and forms can seem a bit bewildering at first, but as soon as you have decided on your wedding style, the officiant in charge – whether it be a registrar, reverend or rabbi – will be able to guide you through the maze of religious and legal requirements. Whatever you do, don't let the official considerations take the fun out of the preparations. Get them sorted early.

The basics

- One partner must have been born a male and one a female.
- Both must be marrying by their own free consent.
- Applicants for marriage should not be blood relatives or close family members (see Who You May Not Marry, page 36).
- Couples must give notice of their intention to marry. For marriage within the Church of England, notice is given via the publication (reading) of the banns. For civil weddings and non-Anglican religious ceremonies, the superintendent registrar will make an entry in the marriage book.
- To be legal, a wedding must be witnessed by two competent adults who are required to sign the register.

Age restrictions

- Both partners must be over the age of 16, although those under 18 in England still need consent from their parents or guardians. (If this is not forthcoming, however, and the couple feels the refusal is unreasonable, there is some room for appeal through the court system, although proper legal advice would have to be sought on the issue.) The Church of England requires parental approval for brides or grooms under 18.
- In Scotland and Northern Ireland, couples under the age of 18 can get married without parental permission.

Where you can marry

Civil weddings must be conducted by a registrar or superintendent registrar. Since the 1994 Marriage Act, civil ceremonies are no longer restricted to register offices but can take place in a variety of approved premises licensed by local authorities for the solemnization of vows. However, the sky really is the limit and in the UK it is still not legal to get married in transit, i.e. on a moving plane, or in places such as a forest where no specific address can be given. This comes from the rule which states that a wedding must be a public affair so that anyone with an objection is able to gain access and raise it. For the same reason, the doors to the church or register office cannot be locked.

Religious ceremonies can take place in any church, synagogue or temple (with some variations) and must be conducted by an authorized minister representing the specific denomination. In all cases other than the Church of England, couples must also make a separate appointment with the local superintendent registrar.

◀ As the law stands, so that weddings remain 'public' events, it is still not possible to marry at a private address without a licence. However, there are plans afoot to change the law so that, in the future, it will be the official that is licensed rather than the venue.

WHO YOU MAY NOT MARRY

It is against the law to marry your:

- Mother or father (birth or adoptive)
- Grandparent or grandchild
- Brother or sister
- Son or daughter (birth or adoptive)
- Father or mother's sister or half-sister
- Father or mother's brother or half-brother
- Sister or half-sister's son or daughter
- Brother or half-brother's son or daughter

Marriage between certain in-laws and step-family members are sometimes allowed, for instance a former father-in-law may marry his son's ex-wife, but only if both the son and the father-in-law's former wife have died. The law on these matters is complex so check thoroughly if you feel there may be a doubtful family connection, even by marriage. By the same token, adoptive children are not permitted to marry their adoptive parents, but it may be allowed between other members of their adoptive family.

Civil ceremonies in England and Wales

Superintendent registrar's certificate

The first step is to contact the superintendent registrar for the district in which you live. The law asks that one of you should have lived in the district a minimum of seven days prior to giving notice. Even if both partners live in the same district, each needs their own superintendent registrar's certificate, so both bride and groom must apply in person to the local office and each is liable for a separate fee. Couples then wait 15 days before the certificates are issued. At the appointment an entry will be made in the marriage notice book stating when and where they plan to marry. Couples usually book the ceremony at this meeting, too, unless they are marrying in a different area, in which case they are likely to have already seen the superintendent registrar in the district in which the ceremony will be held.

MUST KNOW

Registrars do not recognize gender re-assignment, which means a transsexual can still be married according to their birth sex, i.e. a man who has had surgery to become a woman can still legally marry another woman.

▲ When applying for a special licence and stating your reasons for wishing to marry in a particular church, a long-standing family or childhood connection will be viewed more favourably than a desire to marry there because it will look good in the photos.

Registrar's general licence

This allows a marriage to take place anywhere at any time and is usually valid for twelve months. It is usually reserved for cases of serious illness or other special circumstances.

Church of England and Church of Wales

Who can marry in a C. of E. church?

Around a quarter of all marriages in England take place in a Church of England church and these are legal as well as religious ceremonies. If one or both of you live within the parish boundaries of a church, or you are a regular worshipper (usually a minimum of six months) and are on the parish electoral roll, you may ask to be married at the church providing there are no ecclesiastical bars, such as one of you being divorced. (Many Church of England ministers refuse to marry divorced applicants although some elect to sanction re-marriage under their powers as the ceremony's civil officiant rather than as its religious officiant.)

If you choose a church outside the parish in which you live and you are not on the electoral register, you must apply for a special licence stating your reasons. A special licence is approved by the Archbishop of Canterbury and issued by the Faculty Office.

FEES

Fees shown were set on 1 January 2005. They are usually revised at the start of each calendar year.
Publication of banns £18
Banns certificate £12
Common licence £64
Special licence £130
Marriage service £198

Banns or ecclesiastical licence?

The most popular and economical route to marriage in the Church of England is via the reading of the banns. The forthcoming marriage is announced in the church where the ceremony will take place on three consecutive Sundays in the weeks leading up to the wedding. The exact number of weeks before can vary and will be agreed between you and the minister beforehand. The minister will advise you of the dates so that you and friends or family can go along and hear them, although it is not mandatory. The banns give the names of the couple and the parishes in which they live. If one party lives in a different parish, the banns must be read there too, not necessarily on the same Sundays, after which the minister at the second parish will give the couple a banns certificate, which must be passed on to the minister performing the actual ceremony. Although timings vary for the reading of the banns, the wedding must follow within three months of the banns being read out.

Special circumstances

Marriage by common licence

Rather than waiting for the banns to be read, couples who want to marry quickly (perhaps because of illness or because of impending overseas military postings) can appeal to the Faculty Office in London or the local bishop or his surrogate for a common licence. Couples with a valid reason then need wait only one clear day before the licence is issued, although one or other of you must have lived in the parish for at least 15 days. One or both of you must also appear in person to sign a legal declaration that there is no reason why the wedding should not take place.

Superintendent registrar's certificate

In some circumstances, a marriage according to the rights of the Church of England may be solemnized on the authority of a certificate of a superintendent registrar, rather than after the publication of banns or the issuing of a common licence. Contact the General Register Office (GRO) for further details – see 'want to know more', p47.

MUST KNOW

For more information on the legal preliminaries and ceremony details for couples who follow the Hindu, Muslim, Sikh, Buddhist, Greek Orthodox or other faiths, there is a comprehensive listing at www.weddingguide.co.uk.

Roman Catholic weddings

The legal requirements for Roman Catholic weddings are basically the same as those for a civil wedding but couples must obviously apply to the priest as well as the local superintendent registrar. The priest will ask you for any baptism and confirmation certificates, showing proof of your Catholic faith. If you are both Catholic, banns will be published, but if one of you is not, you will need a dispensation from the bishop to allow you to marry in a Catholic church. It is best to speak to the priest about this, leaving as much time as possible, ideally six months, before the wedding. Once you have applied to the local superintendent registrar's office to cover the legal formalities for the ceremony itself, the priest is usually authorized to legally register the marriage at the same time as he performs the religious ceremony. If for some reason he is not, a registrar must also attend the ceremony.

Jewish weddings

As in the Catholic faith, Jewish couples must make two applications to be married – one religious to the rabbi, with supporting documentation to prove the Jewish faith, and one civil via the local superintendent registrar, using the same procedure as you would for a civil ceremony. The major difference between a Jewish ceremony and all others in the UK is that Jewish couples are exempt from the law stating that all weddings should happen between 8am and 6pm, and evening ceremonies after 6pm are popular, although Jewish law bans ceremonies on Fridays and Saturdays. The ceremony is usually held in a synagogue but can also be performed under the traditional *chuppah* in a hotel or other residence.

▼ As for any other religious ceremony, apart from the Church of England one, couples following the Jewish faith must make a separate civil application to a registrar as well as a religious one to their rabbi.

Regional variations

In England and Wales couples can have a religious ceremony in their chosen denomination or a civil ceremony in either a register office or licensed building. Other regions vary.

In Scotland

Couples can have a religious ceremony in a wider variety of premises than England and Wales, including venues which are not normally places of worship. Since the new Marriage (Scotland) Act of 2002, civil weddings can also take place almost anywhere with the minister's agreement. The Church of Scotland is also more open to marrying divorcees, although each case is still judged on its individual merits. Parental consent is not necessary for couples between the ages of 16 and 18.

Civil ceremonies

Both bride and groom must give a marriage notice to the registrar of the district in which they are to be married and the registrar will provide them with a marriage schedule. This usually takes at least 15 days but if it is a second marriage for one or both of you, it is sensible to allow more time; a month or more is advisable.

Religious ceremonies

The legal requirements are the same for religious weddings, except that the bride or groom will need to collect the marriage schedule from the registrar seven days before the marriage and give it to the minister or authorized person conducting the ceremony. Afterwards, it must be signed and returned to the registrar within three days. If one of you is resident in Scotland and the other in England or Wales, you should apply for a certificate of no impediment or a certificate showing that the banns have been read out in a Church of Scotland church.

In Northern Ireland

Civil ceremonies

As in England and Wales, notice must be given to the registrar of marriages for the district. There are two routes, via a registrar's licence or a registrar's certificate, and which you choose will dictate the length of time you will need to be resident in the district.

◄ The rules governing the time and place of religious ceremonies in Scotland are far more flexible than in England and Wales. Civil ceremonies can be held anywhere, and are conducted by the local minister, although a registrar will officiate at a register office wedding.

Registrar's licence

This is issued seven days after the couple has given notice. If both partners live in the same district, one must have lived there for at least 15 days and the other for at least seven. If both partners live in different districts, they must each give notice to their local registrar and must have been resident for at least 15 days. (The registrar for the district in which the wedding is due to take place will need a certificate from the registrar in the other district before the licence can be issued.) The licence means the wedding can take place in any authorized premises within that district, excluding Jewish or Society of Friends' weddings.

Registrar's certificate

Both bride and groom must have lived in their districts for seven days. If they live in different ones, notice must be given to the registrar of each. The certificate, or certificates, will be issued 21 days after notice has been given and copies must be sent to the official conducting the wedding.

▲ Couples in which one or both parties is divorced may find it difficult to enjoy a full religious service through the Church of England or Catholic church, although the decision is usually left with the individual minister and some will make exceptions.

Church of Ireland

Religious ceremonies

For members of the Church of Ireland or other Episcopal or Protestant churches, there are four ways to proceed in Northern Ireland.

Licence

If one or both of you has been resident in the district for seven days, you can apply to the local licensing minister.

Special licence

If couples have a valid and accepted reason, and the bishop's permission, they may be allowed to marry outside their own parishes.

Registrar's certificate

Both bride and groom must have lived in their district for seven days and given notice to the registrar. If they live in different districts, they must apply to each district's registrar and get separate certificates as for a civil ceremony. For a Church of Ireland wedding, one of them must also have been resident in their church parish for at least 14 days.

Banns

As in the Church of England, both partners must be members of the Church of Ireland or another Protestant church and have the banns published on three consecutive Sundays in both parishes if applicable.

Roman Catholic

Religious ceremonies

For weddings in the Catholic faith, couples can either apply for a licence or a registrar's certificate.

Licence

This is issued by a licensor appointed by a bishop.

Registrar's certificate

As outlined in 'civil' and 'Church of Ireland' details. The certificate allows a wedding to take pace in a Roman Catholic church within the given registration district.

Australia

● The minimum age in Australia is 18, although the courts may make an exception in 'exceptional circumstances' if one of the party is under 18, *if* they can prove they are at least 16 and are marrying someone who is at least 18.

● A marriage must be solemnized by or in the presence of an authorized religious or civil celebrant and conducted before two adult witnesses.

● For church weddings, the notification of marriage requirement is met by publishing the banns of marriage at the parish church. For civil weddings, written Notice of Intended Marriage must be given to the celebrant at least one month before the date of the marriage.

● Applicants born in Australia will need a birth certificate or an extract of birth. A person born overseas who wishes to marry in Australia will need a birth certificate or a passport showing the date and place of birth.

● If either party has been married before, a decree absolute or death certificate is required to prove qualification for marriage.

New Zealand

● The minimum age for marriage is 16 with parental consent or 20 without it.

● Couples must be married by a registered marriage celebrant, who can be either a registrar of marriages, a civil celebrant, a church minister or a person connected with an approved organization. A registrar in the location of your chosen venue can supply a list of registered celebrants.

● Couples must apply for a marriage licence from their local Births, Marriages and Deaths office and make a statutory declaration that there is no lawful impediment to their marriage. If they are living in New Zealand, one party must

MUST KNOW

In New Zealand, if one of you has been married before, you will be asked to either:

● Produce evidence of the dissolution, i.e. Divorce/Dissolution Order, when you give notice to the registrar.

● Give the date of death on the Notice of Intended Marriage form. You do not need to produce the death certificate.

make this declaration in the presence of a registrar of marriages. Licences are valid for three months from the date of issue.

● If one or both of you has been married before, you must produce proof of the divorce/ dissolution order. In the case of a deceased partner, you will not be required to produce a death certificate but must give the date of death on the Notice of Intended Marriage.

South Africa

● The minimum age without parental consent is 21. Minors (under 21s who have not been married before) must have written consent.

● Civil marriage must take place in a church or other building used for religious services, or in a public office or private house with open doors, in the presence of at least two witnesses.

● Documentation required includes identity documents or authorized affidavits and birth certificates. Foreign nationals will also need their passport. A final decree of divorce and death certificate (or authorized affidavit) is required for those who have been married before.

Canada

● Each territory has slightly different rules governing legal requirements. However, all but one stipulates the minimum age for marriage is 18. (In British Columbia it is 19.)

● Although Canada has no residency requirements for marriage, the couple must apply for a marriage licence and one of the parties must do this in person.

● The period the couple must wait between applying for the licence and the ceremony can vary from 24 hours to 20 days. In most territories, the licence is valid for a period of three months, although in some areas it can be 30 days.

▼ Marriage laws in South Africa are more complex because, in addition to civil marriage, the Department of Home Affairs recognizes customary marriage. This is defined as 'marriage negotiated, celebrated or concluded according to any of the systems of indigenous African customary law which exist in South Africa, and that this does not include marriage concluded in accordance with Hindu, Muslim or other religious rites'.

Marrying abroad

One in ten celebrations is now a destination wedding, i.e. the bride, groom and whoever else is invited/can afford it jet off overseas. This can be romantic and exotic but steeped in legal paperwork. Check the details first or book through a reputable travel specialist.

Unless you are returning to your mother country to get married or have relatives in your chosen destination who can iron out the formalities, trying to understand the legalities, even the language, of a different culture can add to the stress of organizing a wedding. Nowadays, though, there are plenty of specialist travel companies who can arrange the wedding for you. Check their credentials carefully and establish such things as how many weddings your chosen beachside venue is likely to do in one day. You don't want to be just one in a long line of couples on a confetti conveyor belt.

MUST KNOW

Age restrictions
Minimum age requirements vary so be sure to check if one of you is still in your teens. Australia, the Bahamas, France and Mauritius all require the bride and groom to be 18, for instance, while Fiji, Sri Lanka and Kenya stipulate 21. Some destinations, such as Jamaica, will accept under 18s with legally verified parental consent. Others, such as Las Vegas and Seychelles, will marry under 18s with parental consent and presence.

Residency requirements
In some places, such as Las Vegas, you can get married straight away. Others, such as Fiji and the Seychelles, require a couple to be resident for one working day. In Jamaica it is two working days, in Kenya it is four and in France it is 40. Be sure to understand what the term 'working day' means in your destination.

Medical requirements
Find out whether the country you have chosen makes any medical stipulations or requires certification of inoculation.

Registration
Contact the Office of National Statistics to ensure your wedding is registered in the UK and make sure you get a marriage certificate after the ceremony.

◄ Some wedding insurance packages will cover you for an overseas ceremony and/or reception as if it were taking place in the UK, e.g. if it has to be cancelled through illness. They will sometimes cover a ceremony overseas and a reception back home if the two take place within a certain time frame. However, most will not cover things such as baggage loss, which is usually covered in standard travel policies, so ensure you have both.

Keep it legal

Whatever else you overlook in the excitement, don't forget the relevant documentation that will allow you to get married overseas. This varies from region to region, but suffice to say that if you are divorced or widowed, you will need your previous marriage certificate and decree absolute or the death certificate of your former spouse. Take originals – photocopies will not be sufficient proof. Most places will require your birth certificates, proof of deed poll if you have changed your name, adoption certificates if appropriate, and signed affidavits stating that you are both single and free to marry.

Some places also ask for proof of name, address and occupation and some will require that the documents arrive ahead of you by so many days, so don't just turn up with them and hope for the best. In all cases you will be required to have a full ten-year passport, often with at least six months left to run, and there may be visa considerations, too.

want to know more?

Take it to the next level...

Go to...
▶ **Religious ceremonies** – page 95
▶ **Civil ceremonies** – page 100
▶ **Traditional vows** – page 104

Other sources
▶ **Websites**
   www.cofe.anglican.org
   www.gro.gov.uk
   www.gro-scotland.gov.uk
   www.foreignaffairs.gov.ie
   www.weddingvenues.com
▶ **Births, Marriages and Deaths**
   To find out more about official wedding certificates and how to buy copies go to www.ukbmd.org.uk and click Local BMD

First steps

So much to do, so little time…
or, that's the way it can seem.
With every wedding you have
to start somewhere, so forget
the finer details for now and
just concentrate on the
essentials, such as the who,
where and how? Pick a date,
set a style, choose your
attendants and agree how
much – or how little – you can
actually afford.

▶ Planning a date

Winter, spring, summer or fall, all you have to do is... organize the biggest day of your life. But when is the best time? Around 75 per cent of weddings take place between late spring and early autumn, which means competition is fierce for suppliers.

The minute the engagement is announced, it is tempting to just 'get on with it', but unless you are having a small register office ceremony and a pint in the pub afterwards, putting together a wedding is like producing a film. You need to choose a cast, arrange the costumes, write a script and – most importantly – raise the finance. With the best will in the world, most couples need at least six months, some a year. The simplest way is to choose a season, get out a diary and list all the Saturdays. (Obviously, it doesn't have to be a Saturday and anyone choosing a weekday for a wedding usually has the pick of venues.) Then, simply cross off the Saturdays one-by-one according to work commitments, holidays or birthdays, anniversaries and baby-due dates of close family members or friends. Watch out for major sporting events, too. Many a wedding has been spoiled by the groom's party scouring the venue for a TV in order to watch the US Open. The same consideration should be applied to big race meetings or cultural events, when the demand for hired morning suits shoots up.

Seasonal pros and cons

Spring

For: You're taking a chance with the weather, but providing the day stays dry, you should have plenty of daylight for photos into early evening. It is also unlikely that too many people will be away on holiday.

Against: The wedding season begins in earnest and availability gets tight. In the northern hemisphere, Easter falls in spring and many Anglican ministers will not perform the sacrament of marriage during Lent.

> **TOP TIP**
>
> In the initial excitement, it might seem like a good idea to choose a significant date, such as your parents' anniversary, to mark your wedding, but try to keep it to an event that is specific to you as a couple.

Deciding a date
● Wedding preparations tend to grow to fill the time available. If you have 18 months until your chosen date, it will take 18 months. You could probably make the same arrangements – availability of venues allowing – in six.
● If you have a regular menstrual cycle, use a diary to project ahead. Do you really want to marry in the middle of your period?

Summer
For: In theory the most reliable weather, although this can mean disappointment if you wake up to a rogue storm. There is more scope for picnics, marquees and barbecues.

Against: You'll have to wait longer for availability of venues, caterers and florists and you may pay a premium for high season. Many people take vacations so more date-juggling is needed.

Autumn

▼ When you're envisaging your perfect day, you need to think about more than your dress and veil. Make sure you've told the key players the proposed date well in advance.

For: A sunny autumn day can offer warmth without humidity and outdoor photos are great against autumnal colours. The wedding industry is coming to the end of high season and you may not have to book so far in advance.

Against: The alternative to autumn sun is high winds and storms. Weather is less guaranteed at this time of year so cross your fingers.

Winter
For: Candle-lit weddings are incredibly romantic and there is no real disappointment about the weather because there are no expectations in the first place. Many venues offer discounts.

Against: The wedding industry goes into hibernation and off-the-peg outfits are in shorter supply. In the northern hemisphere, Anglican ministers may refuse to marry you during Advent. Early dusk will cut short your daylight, so consider this when booking the photographer.

Choosing a style

Weddings can be starchy, traditional affairs with strict dress codes or they can be wild parties with a come-as-you-are approach. Discuss different styles with your partner and make sure you both know what you mean by terms such as 'informal'. To some people informal means 'no top hats', to others it means 'no ties'. To the sartorially-challenged it can even say 'shorts welcome'.

Key choices

The initial considerations for any wedding are:
- Religious or civil ceremony with/without a blessing?
- One location or two (many venues licensed for civil ceremonies double up for the reception)?
- Close friends and family only or a general invitation to all?
- Daytime event only or day plus evening party?

The number of civil weddings in the UK now outnumbers religious ones, especially since the laws were relaxed in 1994 to allow ceremonies at places as diverse as football grounds, museums and castles. The choice of ceremony is the most personal thing of all and is one facet of the wedding where you really should not allow yourself to be swayed by others. Some couples don't feel married unless it is in church, others who don't worship regularly – if at all – feel it is hypocritical to suddenly want the use of a church. (Some members of the clergy agree and prefer couples who have expressed an interest in a wedding to express an interest in a few Sundays of morning worship, too, before they agree to marry them.)

PICTURE THIS

If you really don't know whether to go 'big and formal' or 'small and intimate' (or settle on somewhere in between), close your eyes and picture yourself as a bride – the way you used to as a little girl. Can you hear majestic organ music or delicate strings? Is everyone who turns to look at you wearing top hat and tails, or casual jackets and no ties? Is your wedding album full of grand family groups taken in front of ancient wooden doors or are you throwing back your head mid-laugh as you swing a little bridesmaid round by her arms? You probably do know what you want deep down; sometimes you simply have to tap into your subconscious to find it.

Mix and match style

The great thing about the modern wedding is that etiquette is increasingly flexible. It's easy to think that, if you go for the traditional church service, with the long dress and veil, everything else has to be done 'the way it was in the past'. It's a line often taken by traditionally minded mothers and it's an area where you may have to put your foot down. If you don't want to be 'given away' by dad, for instance, many ministers are flexible about who you would like to walk you down the aisle. Bridesmaids are not compulsory if you don't have any conveniently aged nieces and you can usually have more than one best man (or woman) if it's too hard to decide on one.

Beware a theme

If you and your beloved have an unusual history it is tempting to go for a 'themed' wedding. These offer lots of visual originality, but are often better if the ideas grow organically. If you are both members of a local historical society, a medieval flavour can be a great base. However, if you begin your preparations with the idea that every element of your day must fit a specific theme, you may impose frustrating restrictions on yourselves.

▶ For couples not drawn to a religious service, a civil ceremony can offer much more opportunity for creativity. Besides the mandatory wording required by law, there is much more flexibility to incorporate your own personal wording into the vows and readings.

The principal players

Early in the preparations you may face a diplomatic crisis. Who to choose as best man, bridesmaids, pages, ushers and witnesses? Everyone likes to feel involved so, however well you know friends and family, tread carefully...

The best man

Although nominating a best man may look like a 'reward' for being a loyal friend, he needs to be chosen for his organizational skills as much as for his ability to tell jokes. A best man doesn't just give a speech, he marshalls guests, arranges lifts and troubleshoots when there aren't enough vegetarian meals. If there is an obvious candidate, sign him up. If not, consider splitting the duties between two friends. Beware, too, of asking someone shy. The prospect of making a speech may rob him of the ability to sleep for months!

Matron-of-honour or chief bridesmaid?

Unlike the best man, this is not such a specific role and a bride isn't required to have one. (In fact, if your best friend would not relish wearing a long pastel dress, there is nothing to say she can't play the 'matron-of-honour' role in civilian clothes.) Traditionally, the adult bridesmaid closest to the bride was chief bridesmaid and called a matron-of-honour if she was married. She would help with the planning, especially outfits, and help the bride get ready on the day. Officially, she would walk down the aisle beside the best man after the ceremony and sit at the top table with him to equal out the numbers. However, with extended family considerations, it is now quite usual for bridesmaids to sit at their own table and for the best man to be accompanied by his partner at the top table.

Bridesmaids and flower girls

If there are adult and children attendants, the little ones are known as flower girls. How many of each, if any, you have is usually dictated by budget and family pressure, often the latter. The politics of choosing bridesmaids can be fraught, though. Sometimes, by asking one friend's daughter, you feel obliged to ask another and the list goes on. However, if certain children are absolute nightmares, resist pressure to include them. They will take the shine off the day, either by misbehaving or because you will constantly worry about what they are doing.

Usual best man's duties

- Arranging the stag night.
- Overseeing transport/lifts from the ceremony to the reception.
- Trouble-shooting if things go wrong or guests become unruly.
- Settling outstanding bills/taxi fares/cash bar on the day.
- Giving a speech.
- Returning any hired menswear, including the groom's.

Chief bridesmaid's duties

- Arranging shopping trips for dresses, veils and accessories.
- Helping the bride get ready on the day.
- Carrying tissues, spare make-up, scent for the bride.
- Supervising younger attendants, particularly at the start of the ceremony and during the photos.
- Assisting the bride to remove her veil and/or change at the reception.

▼ Never forget the politics of the very young. If nieces and nephews squabble in everyday life, imagine the possible tantrums when they are put in the spotlight.

▲ Most fathers will understand if you want to play down the 'giving away' element of the traditional ceremony but still like to feel involved in some way.

Father of the bride

Customarily this was the man who got to give away the beautiful bride, extend a few warm words of welcome to the guests and then pay for everything. Of the three, only one is really steadfastly followed today, that of making a speech. Many brides prefer not to be 'given away' in the traditional sense, although most still choose to enter the ceremony on their father's arm if they can. The custom of paying for everything has also evolved dramatically, and it is far more common for parents on both sides to share costs or pay for specific elements of the day, such as the wine or the honeymoon, rather than the whole lot.

Father of the groom

In theory, it was the groom's father who issued the bride's parents with an invitation to a getting-to-know-you dinner after the engagement was announced, although this custom is all but forgotten nowadays. Other than that, the groom's father ordered his top hat and tails and took a back seat to enjoy the show. Today it is not unknown for the groom's father to follow the bride and extend a few words of welcome to her family during the speeches.

MUST KNOW

Usual usher duties
- Arriving first at the church to welcome early guests.
- Handing out buttonholes.
- Showing the groom's guests to the right and the bride's to the left.
- Escorting the mother-of-the-bride as well as any elderly single ladies to their seats.
- Distributing orders of service or hymn books.
- Assisting with parking problems.
- Helping the best man arrange spare lifts or taxis to the reception.
- Checking the venue for cameras, umbrellas, jackets and any other misplaced items after the ceremony.

▲ The more ushers you have, the better organized your ceremony should be, whether it be showing guests to their seats, giving out orders of service or hymn books, or even directing guests to the nearest parking spaces.

Ushers

If you are wondering what to do with teenage brothers, cousins and nephews who show zero interest in the wedding preparations, give them a job. It is nice to keep this role in the family, too, as ushers are the first familiar faces that most guests see and it offers guests an immediate reassurance that they are at the right wedding!

Witnesses

After the bride and groom, these are the most important people in the eyes of the law. You can get married without a best man or bridesmaids, but every wedding must comprise five people – the bride, groom, minister/registrar and two witnesses. After you have signed the register, it must be signed by two competent adults and it is diplomatic to choose one from either side. To avoid too many people milling around in a small church, you could nominate a bridesmaid or the best man, as they are already near the front, but as they already have a substantial role, it is a nice opportunity to involve someone else close. Some couples ask both the mums, others siblings or the parents of smaller attendants.

▶ # Agreeing a budget

Whatever your financial means, setting a budget is one of the first – and trickiest – elements of planning a wedding, not least because it is notoriously difficult to stick to, but also because you and your intended may not always agree on the priorities.

In the excitement of announcing your engagement, parents and even grandparents on both sides may express their wish to contribute towards the festivities. (Gone are the days when the bride's parents were expected to foot the bill for everything apart from the church fees and the honeymoon – traditionally the groom's domain – and although some proud dads still offer, it is more usual for costs to be shared with the groom's family or, increasingly, borne by the couple themselves.) Dividing out the costs can be a great way of easing the burden, providing you remember a few rules.

● One family might have a few hundred in mind, another might be prepared to contribute thousands.
● When someone else is signing the cheque, they often feel it gives them the right to decide how it is spent.
● One family might be happy to contribute straight into a general wedding account and leave how it is spent to you; others might want to know specifically what their contribution will be used for, i.e. drinks, flowers, etc.

How to pay?

Establish this very early on. If you both take it in turns to pay deposits as they come up, you will soon lose track of who has paid for what and, as stress levels grow, resentment can creep in. Open a savings account specifically for the wedding or apply for a credit card with an interest-free introductory offer – keep it exclusively for wedding plans, and make a vow to cut it up and clear the balance as soon as possible afterwards. Alternatively, ask about a fixed-interest bank loan, which is likely to be more cost-effective than loading up existing credit cards.

Couples often find their priorities differ. He may want to offer guests a free bar; she might prefer to ask them to buy evening drinks and use the saving on favours instead. He might feel that an extravagant cake would make a fabulous centrepiece; she might have an issue with expensive cakes and think the money would be better spent on an ice sculpture serving chilled vodka.

● To get a rough idea of overall costs you could gather together some estimates, but remember an estimate is only a rough idea of what something might cost depending on season, market fluctuations and numbers involved.

● Before you book anything ask for a proper quote, clearly showing whether VAT is included, whether there is a minimum order or a discount for bulk orders, when a deposit is required and at which point, if at all, it is refundable.

● Consider wedding insurance. These packages are devised specifically to cover against the most common spoilers, from family illness and bereavement, to suppliers going out of business or failing to deliver. Some will even cover you for deposits paid out before the date the policy is activated so it is never too late to consider signing up.

● Agree not to argue over finances and try not to fall into the trap of saying 'well I paid for this, so you can pay for that...' The day is about you as a couple and the investment is for you as a couple. Spending money jointly is a big step and one you're going to have to get used to.

▼ Don't write your first estimate in stone. It will almost certainly change, probably by increasing, so add on between 10 and 15 per cent for good measure.

How much?

The average cost of a wedding in the UK in 2004 was between £14,000 and £15,000. Mention this to your other half and see if he goes pale. If it seems to be close to what he was expecting, then ask him where he thinks the bulk of the money will go. The major costs are still fairly obvious: the clothes (the average bridal gown comes in at around £900–£1000), the reception (catering and drinks), the rings and the honeymoon. Surprise costs include: flowers, which can add up very quickly; bridesmaids' accessories, such as shoes, ribbons or head-dresses; photography, usually because it is the first time most couples have commissioned any; and stationery, especially if you want invitations, orders of service, place names and menus to match.

Saving money

It is a simple fact that the size and style of your wedding will dictate your budget. If you have your heart set on 150 people, you may have to choose a finger or fork buffet rather than a seated meal. If numbers are restricted to 50, the same budget might well run to a five-course banquet.

Keep it small and stylish

If you want eight bridesmaids, three vintage Rolls Royce cars and enough flowers to fill the Albert Hall, you will have to start saving, but nowhere is it written that expensive equals good. Throwing money at a wedding doesn't buy taste or style, so consider doing a little well rather than a lot badly. Most savings will be made at the reception, although there are other areas where money can bleed away.

Flowers

Concentrate on a few bold arrangements and don't try to cover every shelf and window ledge. Bridesmaids don't need massive bouquets, just simple posies, and not everyone needs a buttonhole. Flowers such as roses and lilies eat into the budget, so bulk out arrangements with perfectly lovely (and cheaper) alternatives such as freesias, gerberas and foliage. Ask keen gardeners among your friends what foliage they have in their gardens. It's surprising how effective laurel leaves and ivy can look in church – this doesn't look cheap, it looks personal!

Stationery

RSVP cards are helpful but not necessary, neither are individually printed menus. Instead of ordering them with your stationery, ask a friend with lovely handwriting to copy out one neat menu for the centre of each table instead.

Reception savings

● Not inviting children saves money if you can do it without offending friends. At a small, low-key drinks reception at a restaurant, for instance, children get bored, especially if there is no disco, no distraction and nowhere to run about.

● Be wary of booking a very early ceremony. An all-day summer wedding can be glorious, but you may have to feed your guests more than once.

● Live music, such as a string quartet in the background, is a lovely idea at a reception, but if the budget is running out, put together some CDs of your favourite music instead and play them through the venue's sound system.

● A three-course meal can work out a lot per head. Why not book two courses instead and splash out a little extra on a luxurious chocolate cake, which can double as dessert?

● If champagne is prohibitively expensive, enquire about sparkling wines and disguise with kir or orange juice. Or scrap bubbly altogether and serve jugs of Pimms in summer or mulled wine in winter. Per head it is more economical.

Favours

▼ If you know someone with fabulous handwriting or who is good at calligraphy, call on their services to help you with place names and save on printing costs.

Traditionally the bride and groom left little favours (usually sugared almonds) or similar gifts for their guests, usually on their place settings, but this tradition is not followed so slavishly today. In fact, the quest for originality has seen couples opt for increasingly unique and expensive gifts such as individual miniatures of spirits, handmade soap featuring the scent of their theme flower or even individually-crafted trinket boxes sporting their initials. Another trend has been to leave an individual rose or other flower at the place setting, which is a lovely thought, but costly. These ideas sound special, but with 150 or so guests, the expense can become astronomical. If you want to make a saving here, most people won't notice or care. And don't feel guilty – you are giving people who love you a fabulous party and sharing your happy day with them. Surely that is gift enough?
If you are worried that people won't have a personal memento, put extra thought into the invitation design or order of service.

More than one party

If you have many friends and family, including older relatives and long-standing friends of your parents, you could divide the day rather than trying to invite them all to everything, and keep to a budget at the same time. It does involve a bit of diplomacy and more than one invitation, but it can work.

After the ceremony, why not have an early drinks reception with all the usual elements, such as cutting the cake, speeches and canapés? This will often satisfy the older generation and traditionalists who are not keen on discos. Once the conventional elements are over, older family members and friends of your parents, etc. can leave and you can then have a dinner (the most costly part of any wedding) and dance to which only your closest and more contemporary friends are invited. The other, and more usual, way to split the day is to invite only closest friends and family to the ceremony and wedding breakfast and then open up the guest list in the evening to drinks and dancing. The

▲ Don't be pressured into opting for the most lavish cocktails, the most expensive champagne and the most costly, out-of-season flowers. Think about what you like and what you can afford. White freesias make a relatively inexpensive but lovely, fragrant bouquet.

minus point to doing it this way round is that fewer people actually see you get married and people invited to the evening and not the ceremony can sometimes feel a bit like second-class citizens.

Don't be bullied

You may come across people who believe things should be done a certain way and will make no secret of the fact. These may be suppliers, venue managers, designers or your own mother. If you start off by agreeing with everyone else and trying not to offend them when they make suggestions, you are on the road to disaster. By the time you are nine months down the line, your wedding will have morphed into something that bears absolutely no resemblance to the celebration you may have pictured at the beginning.

Either way, trust your gut instinct and learn to say no. Some suppliers will be born salespeople and as soon as they have reeled you in like a fish, will try to get you to increase your order. You might have been perfectly happy with Menu A, but then they suggest Menu B, which is half the price again but 'so much better'. Remember, it's not better if it's not what you want, and if they give you a withering look as if to imply that you are cutting corners, let them. Better still, hunt around for someone who won't give you a withering look in the first place! With most things there is usually a budget price (the cheapest), a middle price (the average) and the premium rate (the most expensive). The middle price is often a good compromise and is usually anything but average. Don't be tempted to stray too far from your budget and if suppliers pressure you to change your mind about something previously agreed, change your supplier instead.

MUST KNOW

When the pressure is on

- People offer advice because they think you want it. If you don't – tell them.
- Wedding suppliers are working for you, not the other way around. If you hear a florist or caterer say 'I'm really not happy about xx…' run a mile
- The only thing you MUST do at your wedding is enjoy it.

want to know more?

Take it to the next level...

Go to...
- ▶ Catering options – page 70
- ▶ Style setting – page 130
- ▶ On the day – page 164

Other sources
- ▶ To check if there are any big sporting events that will clash with your wedding go to www.uksport.gov.uk or check dates via a ticketing agency such as www.ticketsukltd.com
- ▶ For information on financial planning and budgeting go to the website www.fsa.gov.uk/consumer/ or check the loan comparison tables via the Financial Times online at www.ft.com/yourmoney

Essential

planning

You may already have the big vision for your wedding day, but each detail needs careful planning, from the choice of venue and videographer to the food and the cake. The best advice is to book as early as possible – the most popular and professional suppliers are often in high demand, especially in the spring and summer.

Venues

Your choice of where to exchange vows and celebrate will be dictated by your style of wedding. A civil ceremony can often be held at the same place as the party, whereas, in most cases, a church wedding cannot.

The scene of your big day is as important as the people you invite, yet it is tempting to choose something that is just a backdrop, rather than a functional place to make your dreams come true. However pretty it may look in the pictures, for instance, a tiny, low-ceilinged Norman church is not going to be appropriate if you have 200+ guests in mind and your family all average six foot. Equally, you may adore a lake-side restaurant for your reception, but if you have lots of small children in your family, parents won't enjoy chasing over-excited toddlers beside open water. Secondly, your reception is likely to be the biggest expense of your wedding, so don't compromise by making excuses for things that don't feel right or be panicked into booking something because you might not get anything else. You may have to look at six, eight or even ten places, but you only need one and you'll know when you find it.

Ceremony venues

This will largely be dictated by your faith, if you have one, and your family geography. Once the 'when?' and 'how?' have been decided, it is a case of booking the 'where?'. If you're marrying in church and need to find a reception venue which is also free on your chosen date, make a provisional booking with your minister and ask them to contact you if any other couple shows an interest in your first-choice date. This should give you time to size up reception venues.

MUST KNOW

Safety and restrictions

● Some venues, particularly heritage sites, stately homes and museums, not only ban all smoking, but also red wine.

● Is there a ban on outdoor music, a maximum volume or a time when it has to go off?

● Will you be allowed candles or fireworks, including sparklers?

● Will you require additional public liability insurance?

◄ Think beyond the photographs when choosing venues. Yes, backgrounds have to work well in the pictures, but they also have to suit the size and style of your celebration.

Reception venues

Think logistically and ask practical questions as you look around and address potential sticking points early on.

Questions to ask

- Where would people go when they arrive/have drinks/freshen up?
- Are there enough toilet facilities and do they involve flights of stairs? Would they prove a problem for the elderly (or inebriated)?
- Is there somewhere for smokers and a place away from the music for guests who don't dance and prefer to chat?
- Is it child-friendly and would you be able to put up a bouncy castle, puppet show or some other kind of entertainment?
- Do staff seem flexible to alternative ideas, catering, seating, room usage or are they a bit 'this is the way we do things'?
- Are the kitchens 'well-run'? Ask to have a look.
- What parking facilities are there on the premises or nearby?
- Would you have to share with other weddings or parties on the day and where would any crossover come in?

Marquees

Not everyone has rolling gardens at home, but if it is an option at your chosen venue, a marquee is a fantastic finishing touch for a spring or summer celebration.

Marquees are not a cheap option but they do offer a refreshingly broad canvas, literally, for brides with vision. Although the planning can take on a new, more complicated level (with the need for staff and generators or to build false dance floors, etc), a marquee lets you tailor-make your party.

Which style of marquee?

You will probably be offered one of three choices. The first is the traditional circus-style, big top tent, known as a tension tent, which has the familiar guy ropes and a central pole with a domed roof. This works in most kinds of gardens or fields and offers a great feeling of space. The second is a push-pole tent, again depending on guy ropes, but less taut-looking. The ceiling slopes down from a row of internal poles to perimeter poles. The number of poles can make arranging chairs a little tricky. However, this type is more informal and often available in unusual styles.

◀ A good marquee hire company will be booked up many months in advance, some as far as 18 months for summer weddings, so get your order in quickly, especially because large marquees can take longer than a day (some up to three days) to erect.

EXTRAS TO CONSIDER

- Flooring, lighting and lining are often quoted separately from the initial price.
- If the meal is in the marquee, you will have to hire everything from cutlery and linen to glassware and vases, unless your catering company can supply.
- If the marquee has to be located some distance from a building, toilet facilities can be a problem. You may need portable toilets, which can bring problems of their own, particularly when people have been drinking and it gets dark.
- When approaching friends with beautiful gardens about the possibility of putting up a tent, remember that lawns do not always look so manicured after a day of tent pegs, false walkways and many pairs of stiletto heels.
- Balmy summer days can turn into chilly nights. What insulation/heating options can your company offer?
- If the marquee is some way from the main house or building, will it be left alone for any length of time and will you need some kind of security presence?

The third is a more modern marquee with a self-supporting aluminium or steel frame, which is not only great for uneven ground, but also suitable for hard-standing surfaces, such as courtyards or pathways, and is more hardy in bad weather.

Public liability insurance

A reputable supplier will have public liability insurance. Check this, as more than one tipsy guest has slipped on a dance floor or tumbled over a guy rope. Marquee cover is often an extra premium with wedding insurance policies for much the same reason.

Finding a supplier

Any professional worth their tent pegs will come along and inspect the proposed site before offering a quote. Make sure it is a company which specializes in weddings, and ask for referrals of previous customers. You want elegance, not *Carry On Camping*. Try to give them a true estimate of the numbers involved. Marquee companies have to allow so much per person for seating and table space, plus room for the DJ's decks, dance floor, bar, etc., in order to give you the tent you require. If anything, overestimate the number of guests rather than underestimate. Ask if a member of staff will be on hand for the day – this may cost extra – or for a mobile number in case of emergencies.

The catering

Unless your tastes run to high fashion, food and drink is going to eat into most of your budget, if you'll pardon the pun. However many guests you invite, they will need to be fed and watered, so plan meals and menus with the season and time of day in mind.

The drinks reception is the transition point in any wedding. The formalities are over and now everyone wants to mingle. Traditionally this was done over sherry, but few caterers would advise this in the 21st century. Champagne is the customary drink of celebration and if your budget can only run to a limited number of bottles, serve it early, as your guests' first drink, when their palate is dry and they can really appreciate the flavour. If you save it until the toasts, its distinct taste will be dulled by food, wine served with the meal or other soft or alcoholic drinks.

◄ Bubbly is not the only option for a welcome drink. There are other sparkling wines from outside the Champagne region, which are often more affordable. As an alternative, consider Bellini (fresh puréed peaches, raspberry or other fruits with Prosecco) or Kir Royale (sparkling wine with Cassis).

HOW MUCH ALCOHOL?

- Order more than you need and ask for it on sale-or-return. You will be charged for any bottles opened but not finished.
- On top of champagne, cocktails, etc., allow at least half a bottle to a bottle of wine per person. While some guests will not touch their allocation, there are always others who will exceed theirs! Light white wines rather than strongly-flavoured, oaky ones and fruity reds rather than heavy blends are more popular.
- Don't skimp on mineral water, especially if you are having an afternoon-through-to-evening party, as most people can get through up to a litre alongside alcohol, especially drivers.
- There are six standard glasses of wine per bottle. Ask for wine to be served in smaller 125ml glasses rather than the modern bowl wine glasses, otherwise your budget will be shot in no time and so will your guests!
- Each bottle of champagne will fill between six and eight standard flutes. Don't be too rigid with your calculations. People don't know they are supposed to have only two glasses each. And as people drink more, so they put down their glasses and lose them.
- If you plan a free bar, make a rule that children can use it only if they are accompanied by an adult. Children get excited at the prospect of unlimited Cokes and find it a novelty to order at a grown-up bar. They also lose their drinks easily.

▼ Serve the good Champagne first, before other drinks or foods – however delicious – begin to confuse the palate.

MUST KNOW

To set up a bar at home you'll need: large chiller containers; lots of ice; ice tongs; half a dozen corkscrews and bottle openers, preferably on chains attached to the tables or servers' aprons; cocktail shakers; a cutting board and knife; and lemons, limes and fresh mint. Where to look: if you are buying in bulk for a party at home, take a look at www.wineandbeer.co.uk

What and when?

Drinks only, with exotic canapés

This is often the choice of couples who want a short reception with a small guest list and limited or no children. It works well in a small venue. Caterers serve canapés from trays so there is no need for seating or elaborate buffet tables.

Drinks with a finger buffet

Similar to above, but you need trestle tables, white linen and adequate china for people to help themselves. This is suited to a shorter reception and works without the need for seats as all food is designed in mouthfuls to enable people to stand and mingle as well as eat.

▲ If you're catering at home, do a few dishes well rather than attempting too many options. Devise tasty mouthfuls, such as baskets of exotic chunky breads and little bowls of flavoured dipping oils, that people can enjoy without balancing plates and glasses. Save any more complicated dishes for when your guests are sitting at your beautifully arranged table.

MUST KNOW

Try to avoid:

● Big bowls of fiddly salad, cold pasta and cold rice, which involve serving spoons, plates and mess.

● Anything which guests have to carve themselves, such as whole fish or sides of beef. They can be off-putting.

● Any dishes which ooze oil or butter or flake excessively when guests bite into them as this makes people self-concious.

Drinks with a fork buffet

This is where you must introduce seating as you will be serving hot and more complex dishes, which require a knife and fork. Not everyone is able to balance glass and plate standing up.

Seated buffet

A variation on the above – a full buffet which requires a seat for every guest, and usually hot and cold choices, plus pudding and cheese.

Seated silver service lunch (often called breakfast)

This is where the cost starts to shoot up because you are paying for waiting staff to serve guests individually. This can be two or three courses, costed per head.

Seated silver service dinner/banquet

Similar to above, but later in the day and more elaborate. The meal becomes the focal point of the reception. Generally this is the most expensive way to do it.

What to serve?

Lamb, chicken or turkey and salmon are the most requested main courses for a reason. They are universally popular, easy to get right in large numbers and flexible enough to be jazzed up with interesting sauces and marinades. Remember any vegetarians in your party and guests who may have a food intolerance, although don't get too worked up about it or you will never settle on anything. You could enclose an additional card with your invitations asking for special dietary requirements; put a little line to that effect with any enclosures such as directions, local accommodation, etc.; or just hope that people will tell you. If cousin Blanche forgot to mention she is a vegan with lactose and glucose intolerance, she can hardly be surprised if there is no specially prepared meal for her. Try to be a little creative with the vegetarian option. There is more to the non-meat-eating diet than quiche or mushroom risotto.

MAIN COURSES THAT ARE BEST AVOIDED

- Very bony fish or seafood served in the shell, which is messy to eat.
- Spaghetti, which can be unsightly to eat and ruin outfits.
- Veal, which offends some people, and game or offal, which others find too rich.
- Anything overly garlicky or spicy.

The cake

The traditional 3-tiered, iced cake is said to be modelled on St Bride's spire in London's Fleet Street. However, wedding cakes have evolved and the options today are endless.

Who hasn't been to a wedding where guests struggle to finish the slab of iced fruitcake at the end of a meal? The cake is a custom most couples follow without much thought, yet, with a few tweaks, they can have an innovative design served at a time when guests really enjoy it. The first major change is that cakes don't have to be rich fruit, covered in marzipan and iced, although there are plenty of excellent cake makers who still do this to perfection. Couples are choosing lighter sponge, chocolate, carrot or a mix of one tier of each (the heavier fruit forming the bottom tier).

◄ Ask where the cake will be displayed. Everyone will want to take photos of you cutting it with your new husband, so you don't want it placed against either a dull or overly lit wall or an unattractive pair of 1970s curtains.

How much?

Some brides have an issue with the often heart-stopping cost
of some of these visual feasts, but expensive cakes can pay for
themselves if you double them up as your dessert course. First,
check how much your caterer would charge for a pudding course per
head. Now divide the number of guests into the cost of your expensive
cake and compare it to the first price. If you cut out the caterer's pudding,
now does it look a viable possibility? If you then follow the increasingly
popular trend of having the cake cutting and speeches before the
meal (to save the groom, father of the bride and best man an
agonizing wait until their public speaking turn), the cake can be
cut during the meal, ready to be served with fresh fruit or cream
as dessert.

Other alternatives

In their quest for innovation, some brides are moving away from the
traditional cake altogether and choosing alternatives, such as the
French *croquenbouche* (literally a tower of profiteroles, either covered
in chocolate or a spun sugar cage), or towers of individually iced fairy
cakes, which make a stunning centrepiece to any reception.

Whatever your artistic leanings, however, you need to find the right
cake maker.

FINDING YOUR PROFESSIONAL

- Scour websites and bridal magazines for inspiration before you approach
anyone. Get a good idea of what *you* would like, rather than being led by a cake
maker who wants you to have what *they* make best.
- Politely decline friends' offers to make and/or ice your cake unless you have
first-hand experience (and taste) of their work.
- Ask the cake maker to calculate how many slices you will get from each tier.
If two tiers is enough for 60 people and you have 70 guests, for instance, is
there some way he/she can make you a smaller, cheaper cutting cake to be
kept in the background for the extra ten slices, rather than going to the
expense of a whole extra tier?
- Will the cost include any cake stands, cutting knives, columns to stand
between the tiers, etc., or will you have to hire these separately? Is a deposit
held for their safe return?
- Will the cake maker be decorating the cake and do you want flowers, berries
or fruit? Does he/she need to liaise with your florist to ensure continuity?
- How long can any remaining cake be kept/stored/frozen?

Say it with flowers

Flowers feature in every part of the day – from the bouquets and arrangements at the ceremony, through to table centres at the reception and decoration on the cake. Deciding on a theme, choosing the flowers and colours and getting the timing right takes precision planning.

Finding a professional

Ideally, go by personal recommendation, but if that isn't possible, ring a few florists who advertise in bridal magazines, or visit some shops. If staff are not instantly helpful rule them out. A florist who can't make the effort to win your custom is going to be even less of an asset once they have won your booking! Ask to see photos of actual arrangements they have worked on, too. Alarm bells should ring if they show you tear-sheets from magazines. These may be ideas but they are not examples of work. You will only see the fruits of their labour on the big day itself and that's too late to find out they are not up to scratch.

Well-meaning offers of help

If you are not using a professional, make sure volunteer friends know exactly what they are doing. Having a flair for arranging flowers in a vase is not the same as knowing where to buy bulk amounts at trade prices.

MUST KNOW

If you are ordering flowers to arrange yourself:
- Make sure you know how many blooms come in a wrap (i.e. roses may come in 20s, gerberas in 40s, foliage in 10s or priced per bunch)
- Ask how far in advance certain flowers must be ordered to open at the right time (e.g. freesias) and which blooms tend to wilt overnight, especially if the church heating is likely to be on.
- Ask for price guidelines before you mention how much you'd like to spend. A professional will be able to suggest ways of making your budget stretch.
- If ordering thank-you bouquets for the mothers, consider where and for how long they will be stored. If they will be delivered to the reception early in the morning but not presented until the evening speeches, they may lose their bloom. For this reason, many florists suggest you opt for an exotic plant instead of cut flowers.

Seasonal favourites

If you are watching the budget, ordering flowers out of season can be expensive.

Spring: lily-of-the-valley, lilac, snowball tree, guelder rose, early flowering peony, cherry, apple, lemon and orange blossom, bulb flowers such as daffodil, narcissus, tulip, grape hyacinth, amaryllis and bluebell, forget-me-not, phalaenopsis orchid, honeysuckle, peony, bougainvillea, gerbera, spider chrysanthemum.

Summer: cow parsley, honeysuckle, jasmine, peony, phlox, stock, sweet william, sweet pea, poppy, lavender, sunflower, hydrangea, passion flower, euphorbia, African blue lily, ranunculus, cornflower, stephanotis, delphinium, azalea, freesia, eustoma, eskimo rose.

Autumn: goldenrod, hypericum, yarrow, late-flowering honeysuckle, red hot poker, dahlia, Chinese aster, late flowering sunflowers, montbretia, aster, gladioli, leonardis rose, echinops thistle, hydrangea, eucalyptus.

Winter: Snowdrop, early bulbs such as tulip, hyacinth and amaryllis, hellebore, winter jasmine, berries, forsythia, holly, amaryllis, lilies.

▲ All-year-round blooms include most varieties of rose and lily (e.g. calla and arum), lisianthus, freesia, carnation, gerbera, baby's breath, iris, anemone, snapdragon, orchid, chrysanthemum and bird of paradise.

TOP TIP

Avoid blue flowers in winter as they have a tendency to bleach out in poor light and disappear in photos.

Where to put flowers?

These are the main places to consider:

Flowers for a church ceremony
- Entrance/porch
- Arches or doorways
- Pew ends
- Pulpit or lectern
- The altar (if allowed)
- The font
- Window ledges

Flowers for a register officer ceremony
- Space is often limited and small arrangements are often organized by the staff so check before you make any bookings.

Flowers for a civil ceremony at licensed premises and/or a reception
- Entrance, foyer or where receiving line will be
- Staircases and balconies
- Drinks or presents tables
- The cake (if not done by cake maker)
- Centrepiece for top table
- Centrepiece for guest tables
- Flowers as possible place settings
- Petals for reception tables
- Thank-you flowers during the speeches

▲ Avoid flowers with pollen, which may stain your dress. Ask the florist to remove the stamens if possible. If you have a long journey to the church or ceremony, ask the florist to construct some kind of carrying container and don't pick them out until you have to.

Bouquets

In recent years, bouquet trends have swung between traditional, cascading shower bouquets and simpler, hand-tied posy styles. Bulky arrangements can be dramatic but cumbersome and the weight will drag you down. Be wary of a pure white/cream colour scheme against a similarly-coloured dress. Without some splashes of colour from berries or foliage, your bouquet will get lost in the photos.

TOP TIP

An alternative to structured floral arrangements on pew ends is to tie organza ribbons around some florist's wire and then twist variegated leaves and tiny buds, even daisies, around it.

Who wears a buttonhole?

There is no strict right and wrong. In the past, some couples provided a flower for every guest, often a simple carnation, but as floral tastes became more experimental (buttonholes using orchids, violets or lilies, complemented with eye-catching thistle, eucalyptus pods or hypericum berries), costs began to soar. Remember, men wear a buttonhole on the left and women wear a corsage on the right.

Reception decorations

These must either be low enough for guests to speak above or tall enough to hold conversations underneath. If the budget is tight, consider vases of flowers as opposed to structured arrangements. The blooms will cost the same, but you will not be paying for the florist's time spent on each arrangement. Ask if the venue or florist has some attractive vases you can hire. If you opt for simple flowers on each table, boost the colour quota by scattering the tablecloths with petals of the same shade. Table centres don't have to be floral and if you are feeling creative and have willing helpers, you can make your own arrangements in advance using foliage and berries, or sprayed dried leaves.

◄ Nowadays, particularly at larger weddings, buttonholes are often ordered only for: the groom, the best man, both fathers, grandfathers, brothers, brothers-in-law, ushers, husbands of bridesmaids and anyone doing a reading or performing a musical solo.

The transport

Work out all the logistics of how everyone is going to get from A to B in advance, so that you, and your guests, arrive in style (rather than in a panic).

A lucky few may be able to enjoy a gentle stroll to the church at the end of the lane, but for most couples, more sophisticated modes of transport – from cars and carriages to helicopters or even golf buggies – are required. A standard package was traditionally two cars: one to take the bride's mother and bridesmaids to the ceremony, and one to ferry the bride and her father. The groom was usually left to his own – or the best man's – devices while guests had to fend for themselves. Today, with the growth of stately homes and hotels as licensed premises, the groom often stays at the all-in-one venue the night before and is already *in situ* (as is the bride), so arrangements vary. It is also popular for couples to arrange transportation for guests such as an old red bus or even a boat.

The farther away the hire company is from your location, the more it will cost, as you will invariably be charged mileage/driving time. Try to establish how reliable they are from your initial enquiry. The person you speak to should have a good understanding of how long the drive may take and the mileage/cost. If they sound as if they are making it up as they go along, don't risk it. You don't want to start your wedding without a car.

MUST KNOW

Hiring transport
- A horse and carriage is very romantic but can make slow progress (three miles can take 45 minutes to an hour), especially during busy weekend traffic.
- A vintage sports car may look fabulous, but a soft-top will ruin your hair and a low two-door model will be tricky to get into and out of with a full skirt.
- Plan in advance if you are going to have photos taken with your dad/husband sitting inside the car. Is there plenty of light? Would a dark colour look better against your dress rather than the traditional white/cream?
- Some car companies automatically place flowers on the back shelf. If you are planning photos and you don't want their red carnations to clash with your cream lily theme, have a word in advance. If you are prone to hay fever, ask them to skip the flowers altogether. This is not the time to get itchy eyes.

What about guests?

Generally speaking, guests can find their own way, but if a lot of people have travelled a long way to a strange area, you might want to take some responsibility. This is a task usually delegated to the best man. You could add a line to your invitation enclosures or accommodation list asking anyone who may need help with a lift to get in touch with the best man and leave his email address or phone number. This will give you a good idea of the number of people without cars or knowledge of local public transport systems. You may find you have only a handful of such people and they can be accommodated in spare seats in other guests' cars. If there are a few more than that, consider ordering three or four taxis/mini cabs to be sure that no-one has been left behind. Alternatively, hiring a red bus bedecked with ribbons is amazingly popular now and is a great icebreaker between different groups of guests who previously did not know each other.

TOP TIP

When booking a car, make sure the vehicle you inspect is the one that will pull up outside on the day, not one that is 'similar', and call the company a week or so before the wedding to make sure it is still available and hasn't had a prang.

▼ If you would like your classic car to stick around for a while at the reception for photos, be sure to tell the hire company, who may charge extra for the time.

Photos and videos

After all the months of preparations, you will want a record of the most beautiful day of your life, your glamorous guests and all those brilliant innovations. So choose your photography and video professional with care. There's no rewind button at a wedding.

Just as you choose a dress code and a theme for your reception, so you need to be sure of your style of photography. You'll be looking at your album long after the last specks of confetti have fluttered away. Get it wrong and you will have years to regret the avant-garde approach you chose in a moment of madness, or wish you had gone for more informal group shots. Weddings are one of the rare occasions when more than one branch of the family comes together and almost the only event which blends the past and the present with the future, so it is a shame to spoil the occasion with a few half-hearted or cold-looking photos.

MUST KNOW

Questions to ask
- Is there a back-up photographer and a duplicate set of equipment should the unthinkable happen on the day?
- If you are talking to a large studio, are all the shots you're being shown the work of the person you will see on the day, or the best bits of everyone's work?
- Ask to see an entire wedding, not just edited highlights, so that you can see exactly how the photographer 'tells the story of the day'.
- Will shots be taken on separate rolls of colour film and black and white film or on colour only? Many photographers now shoot everything on colour and let the couple choose which shots are printed in black and white or sepia after the event.
- What will cost extra? Many photographers will remove unsightly electricity pylons that might have crept into shot as part of the deal, but if you want under-eye bags removed, they may start charging.

Choosing a photographer

As with anything, word of mouth is always best, although bear in mind when the person making the recommendation was married. Trends in bridal photography and technology may have moved on, but that 'brilliant' photographer might not have done. What was great in 1985 may not be what you want now. Failing a recommendation, look through bridal magazines or search on the internet.

Most photographers offer set deals. For instance they may have a standard package where they will take a fixed number of shots (for instance 70, of which they will print up perhaps 30 or 40 for the album). There may then be a super or premium package which includes 50 prints from a selection of 100, or a deluxe top-of-the-range package that gives you unlimited shots from which you can choose even more prints. Many will also include the album, digital retouching and an online proofing service in the cost of the package, but check first. Retouching may not include a tummy that looks a bit fat!

▼ Some photographers will only cover the ceremony and drinks reception; others will include the evening reception, too. Make sure you are clear about what is included before you pay a deposit and assume nothing until you have checked all the details.

Choosing a photographic style

Trends have moved away from traditional family line-ups in recent years in favour of more spontaneous, off-the-wall and reportage styles. However, the smart money tends to incorporate a bit of both. Having an entire wedding taken in reportage style (i.e. no-one looking to camera, distance shots of which people are unaware, capturing the mood and details rather than the principal players) can look a bit random. It also means you can't ensure every key family member will be portrayed in the album, especially the older generation who deem these things important. A good mix for an album might include:

Formal family portraits: Including one of the couple with all the attendants, both sets of parents, grandparents and any children from previous relationships. These are the ones your family will want to put in frames – you probably will, too. They may be formal, but they needn't be stiff, so look for a photographer who will be able to relax guests quickly.

Semi-posed groups: These can be less formal and line-up oriented, perhaps posed around a fountain or bench and without everyone looking directly to camera, and often work well with college or work friends.

Spontaneous shots: If the photographer has time (it may be up to you to factor this in), or if your package offers more than one person, a good professional left to roam with a hand-held camera and a zoom lens can capture those golden-moment pictures – a stolen kiss, a guest throwing back their head in laughter, children spinning around in their floaty dresses – which complete an album.

Picking locations

Photos were traditionally taken with a church door in the background or in the grounds of the hotel, but the variety of venues now offers more creativity and flexibility. While you are choosing a venue and visualizing the seating arrangements or the dance floor, etc., make mental notes of good places for photos, such as balconies, staircases, sunken gardens or imposing fireplaces. Better still, ask your photographer to meet you there in advance and plan some shots together.

Consider leaving some single-use cameras on the reception tables with notes asking guests to take their own shots and see the day from their perspective. However, don't go overboard. One camera per table of six to ten people is sufficient, otherwise people can become a bit wasteful and you end up paying developing costs for pictures which are not particularly well thought out.

▲ Check with your official
about copyright restrictions.
It may not be possible to
film inside a church without
paying a fee and you may
not have permission to film
parts of the ceremony or
certain participants, such
as the choir. But of course
there's no restriction on the
number of pics you take of
your friends and family!

Captured on video

You will probably find friends or family bring their
own video recording equipment with them but if
you want a proper film of the day, don't rely on
this alone. Regard any amateur videos as fun
extras but commission a professional, too.
Fellow wedding professionals – venue
managers, florists, photographers, etc. – may be
able to recommend someone, but make sure
you look at plenty of samples of their work and
are clear about the style.

● Make sure you feel comfortable with the
person you are considering. If the talk is all
about them and how they like to work,
remember you are the stars.

● Ask how the finished film will be presented to
you – i.e. will you be able to see it pre-editing?
Will you be able to dictate what is included/cut?

● Will you have a say in the presentation and
soundtracks? (Otherwise you may find the most
wonderful footage of your lives spoiled by
technical gimmickry and cheesy music!)

ESSENTIAL PLANNING

Photo checklist

These are some suggested shots and compositions to help you plan your album, although some will have to be cleared with the official conducting your ceremony.

Bride's preparation at home
- In front of the mirror
- Jokey shot in rollers/dressing gown
- Mother adjusting veil/headdress
- Leaving the house with father
- Climbing into the car/carriage

The ceremony
- Attendants outside ceremony
- Groom with best man
- Groom with ushers/friends
- Bride's arrival at ceremony
- Flower girls scattering petals
- Processional
- Exchanging vows
- Musical soloists
- Readings
- Couple signing register
- Witnesses signing register
- Recessional

After the ceremony groups
- Couple shot close-up
- Couple shot full-length
- Couple with best man
- Couple with bridesmaids
- Couple with both sets of parents
- Couple with groom's family
- Couple with bride's family
- Couple with siblings
- Couple with children
- Couple with grandparents
- Bride with special friends
- Groom with special friends
- College friends

▼ Discuss 'big' shots outside grand buildings. Unless you want to look like little ants against the architecture, it is wise to choose in advance which part of the frontage you would like as background.

● Run through the
checklist with your
photographer
beforehand. He/she
should know what's
feasible in the time
frame.

● Ask what close-up
shots might work – e.g.
rings, bouquets – and
check when is the best
time to take them.

▶ Aerial group shots often
work best because no-one's
head is obscured, as they
can be when photographed
at ground level. Make a
note of potential balconies
or staircases which offer
this option when you select
your venue.

MUST KNOW

● Check what time the
doors to the church or
venue will be open. Most
photographers like to
take close-ups of the
flowers before guests
arrive.

● If you are relying on
natural sunlight to
illuminate your photos,
make sure you compare
the time of day that you
view the venue with the
time you will actually be
there on the day.

● Team/club friends
● Work friends
● Couple leaving in their transport

Reception

● Couple arriving at reception
● Receiving line
● Casual shot of drinks party
● Cutting the cake
● Couple sharing a toast
● Speeches
● First dance
● Throwing the bouquet
● Leaving the party

ESSENTIAL PLANNING

Stationery

Your invitations are the first hint your guests will have of the style of your wedding, so the content and presentation need careful thought.

Classic invitations

Traditionally these were folded cream or white engraved cards. Lettering would be italic or similar, in plain black, silver or gold with no extra graphics and would simply announce who was marrying, where and at what time, with an RSVP in the bottom left-hand corner. These classic designs still look great on anyone's mantelpiece and are usually ordered through a specialist printer. How you proceed largely depends on your budget. Invitations with raised print are more expensive as they are made by pressing the card into an engraved copper plate and it is the cost of engraving the plate which pushes up the price. A slightly cheaper alternative is thermography. During this process, the card is printed, then sprinkled with a special powder which sticks to the lettering and is then baked.

However, there are many innovative styles, including folds and pop-ups, even invitations designed like a 45rpm single superimposed with the couple's image in the style of a rock legend.

MUST KNOW

Orders of service
- These usually include the church, date and minister's details; the key pieces of music, such as the processional; any anthem performed during the signing of the register; any readings; and the hymns – either the full words with verses and chorus, or the hymn book reference number.
- Rather than print them as a booklet, you could see if the basic information will fit on one sheet then roll them like scrolls and tie with organza ribbons. Get someone who is good at tying bows to make them look really professional.

◀ Blank place setting cards can be ordered to complement your stationery theme or you could go for something a little more unusual, which may save you money but be more costly in time. If you have the patience, smooth pebbles painted with the individual first names work well with an understated table theme.

RSVP cards

If you are very organized and the budget can stand it, RSVP cards pull together all the information you will need for the comfort of your guests. You can even have tick boxes which ask for any special dietary requirements and whether or not people need transportation from one venue to another.

Who sends the invitations?

Traditionally these come from the bride's parents, even if they are not footing the bill. However, invitations can come from the mother-of-the-bride alone if she is divorced, or from the mother and her new partner, if he is close to the bride. If parents are divorced, it is acceptable for them to send invitations jointly, but the mother should use her first name, not her ex husband's. So, rather than coming from '*Mr & Mrs David Collins*', the invitation will come from '*Mr David Collins and Mrs Sandra Collins*'. If the bride's father has passed away and her mother has re-married, he can still be included by putting something like '*you are invited to celebrate the wedding of Michael Dougal, son of the late Lance Dougal and Mrs Teresa Knight*'. If she has not re-married, the wording would say '*Michael Dougal, son of the late Lance Dougal and Teresa Dougal*'.

Compiling a gift list

Research by an Internet bank revealed the most popular gifts in the 1970s were fondue sets and hostess trolleys. The 80s saw the rise of the soda maker and food mixer, which were replaced a decade later by lacquer trays and picnic hampers. Today, with so many couples having already set up home together, less practical presents such as art, wine or hot air balloon trips are just as likely to be on the list.

Why should I have a list?

Some couples feel uncomfortable compiling a list but unless your friends and family are all ardent shoppers who totally understand your needs and tastes, guests will appreciate the guidance. A gift list is not greedy, it is simply saying 'if you would like to give us a gift and don't have any ideas, perhaps you would like to choose from here'. Friends can still go off-list if they want to buy something personal, and if you pick items carefully, there should be something to suit everyone's pocket.

QUESTIONS TO ASK

When can we compile our list, when will it go live for guests and when will it close?
Some stores don't like couples to choose too far in advance of the 'active' date because of stock changes and ends-of-line. They want to avoid you picking things which may not be available as your wedding draws nearer.

Can I add items at any time?
This is a useful facility if guests buy more than one item each or all the more reasonable things go quickly.

Will we get updates?
Some stores issue a password so you can check your list's progress online.

What happens if someone chooses something out of stock?
Some stores automatically issue gift vouchers without informing the guest.

Can guests order by phone/via the internet/in person?
You may have guests who would actually prefer to see what they are buying. Others may be perfectly happy to settle the matter online.

Where to start?

You can do it the long way and painstakingly compile your own list, controlled by a friend, sister or mother. Using this method, guests ask for a copy and then inform the 'controller' when they have bought something so it can be ticked off, but be warned that this is a lengthy process and some people inevitably keep the list longer than they should while dithering over their decision. Or you can let the professionals help.

Designer brand

One option is to place your list with a luxury shop or brand. The upside is you can ask for things normally out of your price range; the downside is that you are restricted to this brand only.

Department store

Many stores operate a gift list register. The upside is you can browse the store with a pencil and scanner and choose products from any department, i.e. soft furnishings, furniture, lighting, glass, china, household, bedding, white goods and electrical. Some guests also prefer well-established store names. The downside is you are restricted to products stocked by that store and dependent on their availability.

Specialist gift registry

These can source gifts from many different manufacturers and suppliers. The upside is the choice is wide and they will spend the time tracking down the exact pattern of china, for instance. The downside is that the sheer volume of brochures can make compiling the list a time consuming, if pleasurable, experience. If the company is based in just one showroom, guests may also not be able to get along and actually see what they are buying.

want to know more?

Take it to the next level...

Go to...
▶ **Keeping children occupied** – page 111
▶ **Let us entertain you** – page 114
▶ **Keeping on schedule** – page 116

Other sources
▶ Websites
  Welcome drinks
  www.knowyourcocktails.com
  Flowers and Plants Association
  www.flowers.org.uk
  Directions for guests
  www.multimap.com
  Photography information
  www.kodakweddings.com

ceremony

Whether your celebration will be a traditional religious service or an innovative civil affair, there are certain basic similarities in all weddings. There are procedures that have to be followed, spoken words of commitment which have to be agreed and a bond to be built between you as a couple and the person who will officiate.

▶ # Traditional ceremonies

Each minister or priest adds their own personality to a wedding service but for a traditional Christian ceremony in the UK, there are certain customs and formalities that are universal. However, in most cases it is best not to assume anything but ask your official for clarification instead.

Church of England

Today, despite the growth in civil ceremonies, over a quarter of marriages in England still take place within the setting of a Church of England church. Neither the bride nor groom is obliged to be a committed Christian or worship regularly, although some ministers encourage couples to attend services for a few weeks to show commitment to the parish. The minister may suggest a couple of meetings beforehand to discuss what marriage means to both the bride and groom. On the paperwork front, there is a Banns of Marriage application which must be completed with personal details. You may also be asked for your baptism and/or birth certificates.

◀ Some ministers suggest couples who are not regular church-goers attend services for a few weeks to get a feel for the church and to become comfortable with the person who will conduct the service.

Order of service

You may be asked which version of the marriage service you prefer and
some brides are particular about whether or not they want to 'obey'. The
choices are the service in the Book of Common Prayer (1662), the Series
One service (virtually the same as the Book of Common Prayer of 1928)
and the New Order of Common Worship (2000). The service usually
includes two or three hymns, at least one religious reading and a short
address by the minister, and is based around the following format:

- Processional: the bride's arrival to a specially chosen piece of music
- Welcome by the minister
- First hymn
- The minister asks if anyone knows of any reason why the couple cannot
be married and asks the bride and groom for their agreement to be
married, e.g. 'do you, Cathy, take Ray...?'
- Exchange of vows and blessing of the rings
- Declaration: the minister asks the family and friends to support
the couple
- Second hymn (optional)
- The readings
- The minister's address: most ministers welcome the couple's own
thoughts or a short biography, especially if they do not know them well.
- The registration of the marriage *, often to a choral anthem or
musical solo
- Prayers and Communion, if applicable
- Third hymn
- Recessional: the couple leave together to a specially chosen piece
of music

* This may sometimes take place at the end of the ceremony and
indicates the point at which the couple is legally married

Blessings

There are various reasons (maybe differing beliefs or divorce) why a
couple chooses a civil ceremony followed by a blessing to sanctify their
marriage. Blessings are at the discretion of the minister and have no legal
standing, although they are much like a wedding ceremony, using a
different tense. For instance, the minister may say 'this is the solemn vow
that x and y *have* taken...' to make clear it is a re-affirmation. There is
usually a short address followed by readings and prayers. It is possible to
have hymns and a choir anthem, too, but each church is different so
approach the individual minister.

Church of Scotland

The main distinction with Scottish weddings
is that they can be solemnized at any time of
day and in any place, providing you have the
agreement of the minister. Unlike the Church
of England, where it is usually the groom who
repeats his vows first, in a Church of Scotland
wedding, either the bride or groom can go first.

Other church weddings

For ceremonies not conducted by the Church
of England, in England and Wales both bride
and groom must make an appointment with the
local superintendent registrar and apply for the
appropriate certificate.

If the wedding is to take place in a building
not registered for marriages, there must be
a civil ceremony first to make the marriage
legal. A registrar may have to attend the
wedding if the officiating minister or priest
is not authorized to register weddings (see
Chapter 3).

Methodist, United Reformed and Baptist
weddings are similar to Church of England
ceremonies in format, although usually simpler.

MUST KNOW

Ceremonies

• Certain restrictions may be imposed for weddings during religious
festivals, such as Lent (Shrove Tuesday until Easter) and Advent (the month
leading to Christmas), particularly in a high-Anglican Church. This can
include: a 'no flowers' rule; a ban on certain songs, such as those containing
'Hallelujah'; and bell ringing.

• If there is no choir, be wary of challenging hymns with high choruses or a
wide range. If there are lots of verses, ask your minister which ones are best
left out and if you are not printing an order of service, make sure the minister
announces which verses you will be singing in advance.

• If you are reproducing hymns on your service sheets, check for copyright
holders listed in hymn books and contact them in case a small fee or
acknowledgement is required.

Roman Catholic weddings

If both partners are Roman Catholic, the ceremony is often part of a full Nuptial Mass and Communion, although this is not a requirement. This is unlikely if one of you is a non-Catholic and, in this case, you will need a dispensation for the ceremony to proceed, which you should have arranged with your priest (see Chapter 3) beforehand. The ceremony is largely similar to the Church of England service. There are Bible readings and a sermon, a declaration that there is no lawful reason why the couple may not marry, an exchange of vows and a promise to bring up any children in the Catholic faith. The rings are blessed and there are also prayers and the signing of the register before the recessional music.

Bells, organist and choir

Many churches no longer have bell ringers but if your church does you will probably be charged according to the number of bells/ringers. Large churches may have eight, others six, and some four. If you are marrying in summer, bear in mind that bell ringers and choir members have holidays, so you may be disappointed at a lack of availability. There will be an extra fee for the organist and the choir. Some churches include this in the fee you pay upfront, others will ask for cash on the day. If there is no choir, consider a professional group of singers to boost your noise levels. There is nothing worse than a half-sung hymn and a church of non-churchgoers mouthing the words. If you hope to record the ceremony, the fees for both the organist and any musicians may increase so be sure to tell them your plans. There may also be higher charges to cover copyright fees on the music being played or sung.

▼ If you are not regular worshippers but have permission to marry in church, attending a few services will help you to familiarise yourselves not only with the architecture and the acoustics, but also the ambience.

▶ A question of faith

Always run through civil requirements with a registrar before you plan any ceremony and check that your rabbi, priest or other religious official is authorized to register the marriage, otherwise you will need a registrar to be present.

Jewish ceremonies

Apart from the civil requirements (see Chapter 3), a Jewish ceremony can take place at any time apart from the Sabbath (Friday sunset to Saturday sunset) and does not need to be in a registered building. Unlike a Church of England ceremony, the bride stands on the right and close family often join the couple under the *chuppah*. The groom breaks a glass underfoot, which concludes the ceremony and the couple are escorted to a private room for a few moments, their first as husband and wife, known as *yichud*.

◄ In some ceremonies, men and women sit in different parts of the synagogue or venue depending on whether the couple are marrying according to the Orthodox or Reform faith. The ceremony and vows take place under a *chuppah*, a canopy often made from silk or velvet, decorated with flowers and supported on four poles.

Jewish rituals include:

- **Mikvah** The bride takes part in a ritual cleansing at the synagogue a few days before the wedding to purify her marriage.
- **Bedecking (or bedeken)** The groom lifts the veil to 'check' he is marrying the bride he agreed to marry and she is not a 'substitute'.
- **Seven circles** The bride circles the groom seven times to indicate she is making him the centre of her life.

Hindu ceremonies

There are so many different branches within the Hindu faith that it would be impossible to cover every one. However, some common strands based on the ancient Hindu scriptures (the Vedas) run through them all, whether the wedding is a big, social event or a private family matter. In most Hindu faiths, a priest will study the horoscopes to choose a lucky date for the wedding. The ceremony itself takes place under a canopy called a *mandap*, supported by four pillars to represent the couple's parents.

Hindu rituals include:

- **Circling the holy fire (agni)** As the couple circle the holy fire, sacred blessings are recited for wealth, good health, happiness and prosperity.
- **Hastamilap** The bride and groom's right hands are joined and bound several times with cotton thread, to indicate that while a single thread can be broken, a reinforced thread, like the couple's union, is unbreakable.
- **Saptapadi** This is perhaps the most significant ritual in the ceremony, when the couple take the seven steps towards happiness and make seven vows to symbolize ideals, strength and power, health and fortune, happiness, children, long life and spiritual friendship.

Muslim ceremonies

The Muslim ceremony is not a religious rite as such, but centres on the traditional civil marriage contract called the *Nikah*. The ceremony itself is quite simple and can vary according to the individual cleric or imam. In some instances, men and women may remain in separate rooms or halls. The bride may not even be present to hear the reading of the contract, and traditionally the dowry, which may be announced instead in the presence of the groom, the bride's father and two witnesses, who then go to the women's room and ask the bride if she will accept the groom as her husband. The couple are not given specific vows to recite, although some increasingly choose to exchange pledges. There are usually readings from the Islamic holy book, the Koran.

▶ # Civil ceremonies

Personalized civil ceremonies can now be enjoyed at a number of new, approved premises in England and Wales, along with the traditional register office services.

Approved premises

When the superintendent registrar arrives, he or she will run through the procedure and finalize any payments. The marriage room must be separate from other activities in the building and remain open to the public. As in a religious ceremony, the couple will stand at the front, before the registrar, surrounded by witnesses, family and friends. The basic service is:

● The registrar makes a statement explaining the vows the couple are about to make.
● The bride and groom declare that there is no legal reason why they should not be married and recite any vows they have specially written in agreement with the registrar.
● Rings may be exchanged.
● The couple are pronounced man and wife. Most registrars avoid the 'you may kiss...' statement but may choose to introduce the guests to the new Mr and Mrs Perry instead.
● The couple, two witnesses, the registrar and superintendent registrar sign the register.

Register offices

The ceremony structure is very much as above, although there may be less flexibility with music and readings, as a register office will have other couples following on behind you.

Humanist ceremonies

Humanist ceremonies have no legal status. They can only be held following a standard civil ceremony, but are increasing popular with

> **TOP TIP**
>
> What you may or may not include is up to the superintendent registrar. In some areas, dogs have been allowed to stand as attendants, while other registrars literally had a hairy fit when asked if monkeys could be witnesses. Some will join in the fun of a themed wedding and wear fancy dress or a hat if it is not too extreme. Others feel their role should be more dignified and may decline.

Civil ceremony legalities

● You must inform the registrar local to where you live that you intend to marry, even if this is not where you are planning your wedding. (If you both live in different districts you will have to do this separately – see Chapter 3.) However, the ceremony will be performed by a registrar whose office is nearest to your venue location – which might be neither of the above – so this is the person with whom you may want to build up a rapport.

● When you both give formal notice to the registrar in your home district, this is valid for up to 12 months.

couples of no fixed belief or those from mixed faiths who want to celebrate without religion. The British Humanist Association conducts over 500 ceremonies a year via a network of trained celebrants. These tailor-made weddings have been enjoyed since the 19th century and are popular with couples looking for something personal. They are unstructured weddings where the couple can face their guests if they choose and the venue does not have to be licensed. For couples who love nature and want to celebrate their union outdoors, this is possible if they are willing to risk the elements. Couples drawn to theme weddings often choose humanism – for instance, a marriage conducted in medieval costumes, followed by a display of jousting.

◄ Any place that is licensed for civil weddings must be a permanent structure and have a roof, so a sunken garden or anything which is on the move is out. The venue you choose may well have a room that is recommended for the service.

▶ Music to your ears

When it comes to music choices, think about the content and lyrics as well as the tune. Many stirring operatic pieces were originally written to portray tragedy or gloom on stage and are not really appropriate for a happy occasion.

Church ceremonies

These are only popular suggestions, but could equally be used in different parts of the ceremony.

As guests arrive: *Sheep May Safely Graze*, Bach; *Nimrod* from the *Enigma Variations*, Elgar; *Hornpipe In F, Coro, Minuet No.2*, Handel; *Air On A G String*, Bach; *Largo* from the *New World Symphony*, Dvorak; *Canon In D*, Pachelbel; *Jesu Joy Of Man's Desiring*, Bach; *Wedding Cantata*, Bach.

Processional: *Trumpet Voluntary*, Jeremiah Clarke; *Trumpet Tune*, Charpentier; *Wedding March* from the *Marriage of Figaro*, Mozart; *Hallelujah Chorus*, Beethoven; *Grand March* from *Aida*, Verdi; *Wedding March* from *Lohengrin* (*Here Comes The Bride*), Wagner; *Fantasia In G*, Bach; *Sleepers Awake*, Bach.

Signing the register: *Christ Has No Body Now But Yours*, David Ogden; *Air* from *Water Music*, Handel; *Romanze* from *Eine Kleine Nachtmusik*, Mozart; *Set Me As A Seal Upon Thy Heart*, Walton; *Reverie*, Debussy; *Songs For Female Voices*, Brahms.

Soloist pieces: *Ave Maria*, Bach; *Ave Maria*, Gounod; *Let The Bright Seraphim*, Handel; *He Shall Feed His Flock*, Handel; *Laudate Dominum*, Mozart; *Ave Maria*, Schubert.

Recessional: *Pomp And Circumstance March No. 4*, Elgar; *Carillon-Sortie*, Mulet; *Wedding March* from *Midsummer Night's Dream*, Mendelssohn; Gospel rendition of *O Happy Day*; *Wedding March*, Purcell; *Trumpet Tune And Air*, Purcell; *Crown Imperial*, Walton; *Arrival Of The Queen Of Sheba*, Handel; *Toccata*, Widor; *Coronation March*, Walton; *Spring* from *The Four Seasons*, Vivaldi.

Civil ceremonies

Many registrars discourage couples from having live musical performances at the brief register office ceremony because of space and time constrictions, but there is nothing to stop you having bagpipes or a trumpeter outside. Live performers are often booked for ceremonies at approved premises, where there is time to set an atmosphere.

▲ At civil ceremonies, it is increasingly popular to choose music from a particular period to suit the age of the venue, such as medieval, Tudor or Regency, providing nothing with church or religious overtones is played.

As in a religious ceremony, popular music for the arrival includes the *Trumpet Voluntary* by Jeremiah Clarke, and *The Hornpipe* from Handel's Water Music for the recessional. However, check with your registrar in case the music you like has hidden spiritual overtones. *The Queen Of Sheba* by Purcell is popular with couples planning civil ceremonies, for instance, although some registrars will object because it has links to the Book of Solomon. Another objection can be Wagner's *Wedding March* from *Lohengrin* because on stage it is set in a religious context, although flexible registrars will let it pass. During the ceremony/ signing of the register, suitable music includes *Orinoco Flow* by Enya and *The Flower Duet* from *Lakme* by Delibes (the haunting music from the old British Airways ads). Of course, classical music is not de rigueur and couples have been known to sign their register to Shania Twain, Van Morrison or even Aerosmith. Other classics include *At Last*, Etta James; *My Baby Just Cares For Me*, Nina Simone; and *The Very Thought Of You*, Nat King Cole.

The vows

Although civil ceremonies are fertile ground for creating your own, heart-felt pledges, you are required, by law, to: 'solemnly declare that I know not of any lawful impediment why I, Catherine, may not be joined in matrimony to Ray...'. This is followed by the contracting words where you call upon those present to witness your vows.

Set in stone?

Obviously in a religious ceremony, there are pledges which have been passed down over the centuries. Ask if there is any flexibility at all. It may be that you can add some sentiments, rather than replace the existing vows, which are, virtually, set in stone. Most ministers of religion are tied by what can be said and certainly in the Church of England and Roman Catholic service there is little room for manoeuvre. However, you can always study the vows and promises from other religions to get inspiration for readings or additional private pledges, or even have them printed and used as table decorations at your reception afterwards.

Writing your own vows

The registrar, or celebrant in the case of a humanist wedding, will have to approve your personal vows, but here are a few guidelines to help you frame your feelings.
● Borrow and paraphrase from traditional vows, removing any spiritual references.
● Try to use variations on the same sentiment, to avoid repetition, i.e. pledge, vow and promise all mean more or less the same, as do attempt, try and endeavour.
● Key themes to incorporate include trust, loyalty, fidelity and faithfulness; support, sharing, friendship and companionship; the ups and

TOP TIP

If you are customising your own vows or writing them from scratch, your assembled guests may be a little confused. So, why not have them printed on sheets of paper to match your stationery theme, and roll them into scrolls tied with ribbon for your flower girls or page boys to give out beforehand?

◄ Many officials will advise you not to learn your vows off by heart unless you are guaranteed to keep a cool head. If you forget them in the heat of the moment, you will be required to start again and will easily become flustered.

downs of any marriage; love, passion and romance; the future, longevity and forever.

● Humour has its place and if you are both crazy about a particular hobby or sport (and everyone knows you are), a play on words to reflect your own personalities makes the ceremony very unique.

● If one or both of you has children, try to include them in the vows with references to the new family unit, naming them personally. If the official has no objection, you could ask for a vow which involves them pledging their support.

● There is an unlimited source of inspiration in song lyrics, famous quotations, proverbs and poetry so make use of the internet. Simply search for 'romantic verse' or 'famous quotations on love'. The difficulty will be in whittling them down to a few. If you plan to print any, technically speaking you should check for possible copyright infringements.

The readings

Church weddings.

Invariably the main reading for a religious ceremony will be from the scriptures. Many Church of England ceremonies, for instance, will only stipulate one reading, and it is likely that your vicar will have print-outs of the most popular from which you can choose. Once you have fulfilled the criteria of having a piece from the scriptures, some ministers are happy for you to have a second, secular reading, such as Emily Dickinson, Shakespeare, one of the Romantic poets or even A. A. Milne.

TOP TIP

Beautiful lines from across the world:

Traditional Hindu:
Now two are becoming one.
The black night is scattered.
The Eastern sky grows bright.
At last the great day has come.

Hawaiian marriage prayer:
I enter into this marriage with you knowing that
  the true magic of love
Is not to avoid changes, but to navigate them
  successfully.

Traditional Irish:
You are the star of each night,
You are the brightness of each morning,

Celtic spiritual blessing:
Now there is no loneliness for us.
Now we are two bodies but only one life.

Apache Indian blessing:
I am the word and you are the melody.

Hindu promise, Baha'i faith:
Like a star should your love be constant.
Like a stone should your love be firm.

▼ There is nothing to say that you can't nominate a favourite bible passage of your own (some brides like to choose the passage that was read at their parents' wedding for instance), but you will have to get the extract approved by the minister first.

YOUR CEREMONY

Ministers often suggest the following:

Psalms

- Psalm 23 *The Lord is my Shepherd*
- Psalm 37 *Put thou thy trust in the Lord*
- Psalm 84 *How lovely is your dwelling place*
- Psalm 128 *Blessed are all they that fear the Lord and walk in his ways*
- Psalm 139 *O Lord you have searched me*

Old Testament and Apocrypha

- Genesis 1: 26–31 *Then God said 'let us make humankind in our image'*
- Song of Solomon 2: 10–13 *My Beloved speaks and says to me*

Epistles

- 1 Corinthians: 13 *If I speak in the tongue of mortals...*
- Colossians 3: 12–17 *As God's chosen ones...*
- Ephesians 3: 14–end *I bow my knees before the Father...*
- Ephesians 4: 1–6 *I, the prisoner in the Lord...*
- Philippians 4: 4–9 *Rejoice in the Lord always...*
- Romans 8: 31–35, 37–39 *What then are we to say about these things?*
- Romans 12: 1, 2, 9–13 *I appeal to you therefore, brothers and sisters...*

Gospels

- John 2: 1–11 *On the third day there was a wedding in Cana...*
- John 3: 18–end *Little children, let us love...*
- John 4: 7–12 *Beloved, let us love one another...*
- John 15. 1–8 *Jesus said to his disciples 'I am the true vine...'*
- John 15: 9–17 *Jesus said to his disciples 'As the father has loved me...'*
- Matthew 5: 1–10 *When Jesus saw the crowds...*
- Mark 10: 6–9, 13–16 *Jesus said 'From the beginning of creation...'*

MUST KNOW

Readings for civil weddings

- The choice of readings is endless providing your registrar approves.
- Popular choices include Lord Byron, *She walks in beauty...*; Elizabeth Barrett Browning, *How do I love thee*; Rumi, *The minute I heard my first love story*; Jane Wells, *Let your love be stronger than your hate or anger.*

want to know more?

Take it to the next level...

Go to...

▶ Music – page 102
▶ Vows – page 104
▶ Readings – page 106

Other sources

▶ Church of England Series One service and Common Worship service booklets can be ordered from:
The Church House bookshop, 31 Great Smith Street, London, SW1P 3BN
020 7898 1300
www.cofe.org.uk
▶ Scottish ceremonies
www.churchofscotland.org.uk
www.siliconglen.com/culture/wedding

Your

reception

Congratulations. You've made your wedding vows, shed a tear and now…you're married. Next stop is the reception, where the serious fun will begin and most of your budget will be spent, so spend it wisely and make sure you have everything covered (and we don't just mean the dining tables).

Your reception

Once the legalities are over, it is time to relax, but make sure you have every angle covered so that you can kick your shoes off rather than kick yourself for something you've forgotten.

Crucial decisions

If you put in the time beforehand, a wedding reception should run like clockwork, leaving you free to celebrate with loved ones. One of the key decisions is to establish who is running the show. This could be the venue manager or event co-ordinator who is probably best placed to know how to pace a drinks reception before the champagne starts to run out and how long it takes to rally and seat guests and serve various courses. If, on the other hand, the venue management seem to want to take your lead on the scheduling, you will either have to nominate/hire a master of ceremonies, or brief your best man well.

If you are hiring an outside toastmaster or master of ceremonies, it may be a good idea to have your best man with you at the time. This way they can work out between them when and where announcements will be made and decide who will be watching the clock and liaising with

---

MUST KNOW

Children's entertainment

● A clown, puppet show or magician can be a good idea, but time it sensibly, so that there is something for children to look forward to, but not so late that they spend all afternoon asking 'when is the magician coming?'.

● A bouncy castle can be a good diversion with two drawbacks a) children drink too much fizz and get sick and b) an adult has to be prepared to keep safety watch at all times. Consider a specialist wedding crèche service if you really want your guests with children to relax and enjoy themselves.

● A simpler, and cheaper, option is to set aside a big table covered with pencils, colouring books, sticker books, some toy farm animals and a few games and let the children gravitate to their own 'corner' naturally.

● You could leave goody bags at the children's places with simple games, pencils and bubbles. In fact, why not ask older children who are not so easily fobbed off with a party popper to plan the contents and arrange and run a 'kids' table at the party. There is nothing like a little responsibility and self-importance to keep the 10+ age group occupied.

◀ Make sure you check with the venue staff how long an average course takes to serve and who will announce when it is time to be seated or time for speeches, etc.

the venue management. Remember the crucial difference between the two. The hired man can only act on what you tell him coupled with prior experience. Your best man, on the other hand, probably knows a number of the people concerned, so may be a better judge of the party mood.

Keeping children occupied

You may feel that there is no place for small children at your reception, in which case make this clear to everyone from the start and stand firm. Children can be disruptive, draining and sometimes wreck a good party. If everyone is welcome, consider some form of entertainment.

Receiving lines

Some brides like a line to focus themselves after the ceremony. If you have a lot of guests, it may be the only time you get to chat with them. Conversely, a receiving line can take forever. Traditionally, it involved a cast of thousands – both sets of parents, best man and chief bridesmaid – but you can cut this to just you and your husband to greet arriving guests.

▶ Decorative ideas

When it comes to personal touches, the division of labour will depend on where you are, the time you have and who is in your team, yet even the smallest of touches can personalize a party and have guests talking about it for weeks.

Table names

Anyone can have numbered tables, but couples are increasingly substituting figures with themed names to suit their history or hobbies. (This also avoids the inevitable sniffy reaction by guests who feel snubbed if they are on table six, not table one.) Song titles or lyrics, football teams, fashion designers, battleships (chosen by one couple in the Royal Navy!) or romantic quotations can prove an icebreaker. Even lines from popular films can work, such as Woody Allen's immortal line from *Manhattan*: 'People should mate for life, like pigeons and Catholics...'.

ESCORT CARDS

In the USA, the escort card is popular. This is where every guest is given a small envelope showing their name on the front. Inside is their table number or name and they can choose to sit wherever they like around that table. This is a semi-formal seating plan that cuts out the headache of who should sit with whom. The cards are often laid on a table strewn with petals or handed out by venue staff on large silver trays as the guests arrive.

Table centres

Traditionally this would be a floral decoration – either tall enough for guests to chat beneath or low enough for them to talk above. However, candles, arrangements of fruit, heavy jars of shells or pebbles and coloured water, and even tanks containing tropical fish have become increasingly popular. Another popular idea is to have tall metal photo holders holding a collage of baby photos of you and your man or courtship pictures to 'tell your story'.

A few suggestions:

● For a rich winter decoration, stand thick white church candles in an arrangement of plums or lychees, topped with ivy or mistletoe.
● Float scented night-lights in a bowl of coloured water set on a bed of flowers or petals.
● Slice the bottom of halved, hollowed oranges (so they don't wobble) and fill with night-lights.
● Flower towers can be made from bamboo 'roped together' with grasses and foliage.

Place names

Your stationery provider will probably have small white or decorative place name cards to fit in with your invitation theme. However, there are other imaginative ways to tell people where they are sitting. You can use ceramic eggs or large laurel leaves. Some brides like to bake special biscuits and ice the guest's initials on top or double the place settings with little favours, such as miniature bottles of spirits tied with parcel labels or small potted bulbs with the name on a gardening label. Candles, wire photo holders or a single flower also work well in this way. Or why not simply use pretty labels or ribbons containing the guest names to wrap around each napkin, finished with a sprig of rosemary?

As your imagination runs riot, however, try to remember that for every new level of decoration or innovation you introduce, someone will have to take responsibility for buying the bits and pieces, preparing them beforehand and ensuring they are arranged in the right place on the day.

▼ If you have booked a stately home or hotel, the venue will probably look after your table decorations in co-operation with your florist. If your party is in a marquee in a friend's or relative's garden, you will have to organize every candle and vase yourself.

Let us entertain you

Drinks loosen people's inhibitions, food revives their energy levels and then they are ready to be entertained. Whether you and your husband wow them with a dance display, engage a jazz band or hire a DJ, don't let the party fall flat.

Gee, they got a band

Unless you are providing background CDs (and couples at smaller venues are increasingly choosing this option to keep things personal – just check their sound system first), you will probably want some musical distraction. If you fancy a gentle accompaniment to dinner followed by lively dancing afterwards, try one of the many entertainment agencies, who may be able to do you a deal on a string quartet followed by a band later. Don't underestimate the level of chatter, however. Many a lone pianist or harpist has been drowned out during drinks or a meal by the excited noise of 100+ guests. Today there is no limit to originality (if the budget can stand it) and couples are increasingly considering visual entertainment such as dancers (Cossack, Greek, even Morris), belly dancers, gymnastic displays, Las Vegas showgirl routines, mime artists and comedy acts. Just be mindful of offending youngsters or the older generation.

Popular first dances

A *Wedding Day* magazine poll among DJs revealed some of the most requested artists and songs included:

- Van Morrison *Have I Told You Lately?, Someone Like You, Brown Eyed Girl*
- Shania Twain *You're Still The One*
- Louis Armstrong *Wonderful World, We Have All The Time In The World*
- Frank Sinatra *You Make Me Feel So Young, Fly Me To The Moon*
- Nat King Cole *Let's Face The Music And Dance, Let There Be Love*
- Eric Clapton *Wonderful Tonight*
- Wet, Wet, Wet *Love Is All Around*
- Al Green *Let's Stay Together*
- Harry Connick Jnr *It Had To Be You*
- Real Thing *You To Me Are Everything*
- Tony Bennett *The Way You Look Tonight*
- Elvis Costello *She*
- Simply Red *The Air That I Breathe*
- Elvis *The Wonder Of You*

Audience participation

Karaoke is probably not a good idea because it takes the emphasis away from the couple of the day. However, if you do have a good singer among friends or family, you could run the idea past your band of them dedicating one song to you. Equally, if there is a piano at your chosen venue, maybe in the foyer or bar, and the management are happy for it to be used, ask a gifted pianist among your guests to play a few tunes while guests are arriving. This is sometimes a way of involving a family member with no other specific role, but be warned that a few minutes in the spotlight can bring out the diva in the most unassuming of people!

▲ Look for a DJ who is prepared to stray from the playlist, too. If everyone is really rocking to some old sixties stuff, you want a DJ who can keep the mood going with more of the same, not one who kills it dead with slow tracks.

You should be dancing

By now it must be clear that personal recommendation is almost always the best way to find a supplier and DJs are no exception. Be careful to find one that suits your style. Someone who boasts 25 years of experience and believes that *Brown Sugar* by the Rolling Stones is the pinnacle of any night's entertainment may not be as 'cutting edge' as you might like. Equally, a trendy young DJ keen on techno and garage bands may not suit your middle-of-the road forty-something audience ready for some Beatles and Frank Sinatra.

MUST KNOW

Things to ask a band or DJ:
● What time does the fee run until? Are they prepared to stay later and do they charge by the hour thereafter?
● How much time do they need to set up so that you can warn the venue?
● Are all lights and any smoke effects covered in the price?
● Do they offer light projection (lasers and strobe effects)?
● Can they offer you a rough playlist in advance – i.e. two dozen artists/bands they consider appropriate for your style of function?

Keeping on schedule

Certain things need to be done within certain time frames. Imagine your ceremony is at 2pm followed by drinks, dinner and a hotel disco. How may this affect your reception timing?

Planning the day

2pm	The vicar has told you the ceremony will last 30–40 minutes, so you are hoping to be outside and starting photos by 2.40pm. If you allow three-quarters of an hour for photos, plus 15 minutes for kissing and hugging, you can expect to be on your way to the reception (about 15 minutes drive) by 3.40pm, to arrive at 4pm.	Potential delays here include the bride arriving late and the ceremony running over, the photographer taking a long time over light readings, etc. and every guest wanting to congratulate you.
4pm	The bride and groom arrive at the reception while guests follow on and find parking spaces (don't forget you'll just breeze up in your hired car). Time to freshen up, visit the toilet and check the decorations and table arrangements. Pour yourself a drink and put on your best smile.	Potential delays here are traffic or lots of guests having a problem with parking.
4.15pm	Guests begin to arrive (maybe start your receiving line?) and drinks are served. This is a good opportunity to take more photos, maybe just couple shots and close friends, while the ambience is lively and no-one will notice you've disappeared.	Potential delays include guests wanting the washroom facilities. Allow about an hour only for drinks as most guests will not have eaten since long before your 2pm ceremony and the alcohol will go straight to their bloodstream.

During your evening reception, don't try to open gifts and thank guests or speak at length to absolutely everyone, because the night will speed by. Enjoy yourself instead!

5.15 –5.30pm	Guests are called to their seats. This may be when you choose to cut your cake and have early speeches, as is becoming increasingly popular (about half an hour). If not, the meal will probably take a good hour and a half.	Potential delays include guests taking ages to find their seats, no matter how clear you made your table plan.
7–7.30pm	The dessert course of the meal, if you are having the speeches first, or the speeches and cake-cutting if not.	Potential delays are obvious – speakers with too much to say.
7.30–8pm	The transition period between day and evening entertainment. Make sure you and your husband do plenty of socialising or pose with guests for a few informal photos.	Potential delays: guests invited for the evening may arrive, older guests may bid farewell and the atmosphere is in danger of taking a dip as people mill around unsure of where to go.
8pm	Start music and dancing or entertainment. This is where all the five minutes late here and ten minutes late there add up.	Your DJ may be ready at 8pm, but it could be 9pm before everyone is ready for him! If you have a music licence until 1am it will make little difference – if it all has to shut at 11pm, you may wish you'd kept to the schedule.

The speeches

The chink of a spoon against a glass and the hush of voices usually herald the speeches – a moment anticipated with great excitement by the guests (and often dreaded by the speakers). Yet even the most nervous novice can survive his five minutes centre stage with a little preparation.

Who actually speaks?

Traditionally the speeches open with the bride's father or a close relative, such as an uncle or brother who has known the bride for years. This stems from a time when the bride's father paid for most, if not all, of the day and even if the couple have financed the entire wedding themselves, it is still appropriate for him to speak. He is usually followed by the groom and finally the best man. If the bride wants to add a few comments, her turn usually comes after her new husband and before the best man.

The father-of-the-bride

The father-of-the-bride usually shares his sense of pride on this special day and adds an anecdote from the bride's childhood. Then he simply welcomes the groom into the family, wishes the newlyweds much future happiness and concludes by toasting them. If, more unusually, the groom's father has contributed to the cost of the wedding, it is a thoughtful gesture for the bride's father to acknowledge this and invite him to respond. But warn him first – few people can speak off-the-cuff. Remember, too, that there is no rule that the first speaker has to be male. Some brides ask their mother to walk them down the aisle and there is no reason why she shouldn't make the opening speech either.

The groom

The second speech is made by the groom, who replies to the toast on behalf of 'my wife and I' and thanks all the guests for coming. The groom also pays tribute to both sets of parents and whoever else has contributed to the costs of the day, and highlights anyone who has been particularly helpful during the planning. (This is a potential minefield for unintentional snubs so this part of the speech, at least, should be vetted by the bride or written together.) This is also a good time to present gifts or flowers to bridesmaids, mums, ushers and the best man. The groom closes his speech by complimenting the bridesmaids and toasting them.

Many best men
forget that they
have been chosen
for their closeness
to the groom, so it is
not a bad idea to say
something sincere in
your speech.

The best man

The final speech is traditionally the best man
who, officially, thanks the couple for choosing
him and replies with thanks on behalf of the
bridesmaids. He can also thank the hosts on
behalf of the guests and read any cards from
family overseas or guests that were unable to
attend. In days gone by this would have been
the time to read any telegrams. However, as
the telegram has been usurped by e-mail, it is a
good idea for the best man to ask the bride and
groom in advance whether they have received
any that they would like him to read out.

Of course, after the formalities are out of the
way, the real task of the best man is to be
funny, or at least, vaguely humorous. Many
best man speeches hang on the alleged high
jinks of the stag night and this is okay, providing
this doesn't dominate the speech. Remember,
the stag night didn't include the bride and, as
this is her big day also, ten minutes of nudge-
nudge and wink-wink about how much
everyone drunk and how they all got home can
get a bit tedious.

MUST KNOW

Hints to drop to your best man

- In-jokes rarely work. You are trying to entertain too many generations from
too many different sources. Work gags will be lost on relatives and vice versa.
- Know your audience. If double entendres or smutty puns are likely to
offend or embarrass certain people, particularly principal players such as the
mothers, don't include them.
- Never include references to former partners or spouses, particularly if the
children from previous relationships are present.
- Don't go on forever. Five minutes is adequate for someone unaccustomed
to public speaking. Ten minutes is okay if you are skilled at keeping an
audience's attention. Half an hour is stealing the show.
- A quick discussion about the content is not a bad idea, to avoid any nasty
surprises on the day. This flags up any subjects which a best man might
want to include, but which the couple might find objectionable.

Scheduling the speeches

Traditionally the speeches came at the end of the seated meal, after the couple had cut the cake and it was being sliced behind the scenes by the caterers. However, there is nothing that dictates the speeches have to be scheduled with the cake-cutting and nothing to state this has to be after the meal. Many couples are increasingly choosing to do the speeches at the beginning of the reception, before the meal. There are good reasons for this:

● For a dad or best man who is very nervous (the term for a fear of public speaking is glossophobia) it just prolongs the agony. They neither enjoy the reception nor taste any of the food properly because they are anxious to 'get it over with'.

● As the meal progresses, there is a temptation to drink too much alcohol as Dutch courage.

● Early speeches help nurture a friendly environment, and introduce the people on the top table to guests who may be unfamiliar with bride or groom's family. It also gives people seated at tables with strangers something to chat about to break the ice.

● If you do decide to have the speeches earlier, make sure the serving staff are aware of your plans so they can time drinks and courses and know when to call everyone's attention.

LADIES AND GENTLEMAN...THE BRIDE

Although speeches have traditionally been an all-male affair, today the bride and even her chief bridesmaid may like to make a few observations – often to the startled surprise of her new husband. (It is a good idea to tell the master of ceremonies or toastmaster you are breaking with traditions, so that he knows to announce it.) If you want to mark the occasion but are not sure who there is left to thank, an extract of poetry or a funny piece of verse is always well received. Some brides like to propose a touching toast to absent friends or loved ones who have passed away.

Overcoming nerves

- Don't see public speaking as an ordeal. Remember, you are surrounded by friends and family who wish you well.
- Do keep body language relaxed and voice pitch level. When it comes to impact, *what* you say counts for less than 10% of your delivery.
- Don't rush. There is no rewind facility and if you mumble, guests will miss what you say, while everyone whispers 'what was that?'.
- Do imagine you are speaking to one person, not a roomful, but look around constantly so that your gaze doesn't rest on one person for too long.

Delivering a speech

Whoever is speaking – the groom, the best man, the bride or her father – delivery is important. Even if you intend to learn it off by heart, it is worth writing out a speech in full and reading it through a few times. The time it takes to deliver a speech can be misleading – you may have laboured for days over the two sheets of A4, but it could be over in less than a minute. If you are going to read it out, hold the notes high or you will be speaking to the table. If you want to learn it by heart, take the script along anyway in case you freeze midway. A compromise is to plan your speech in full and write reminders of the basic themes on cue cards, such as 'thank so-and-so' or 'remind everyone about the romantic proposal'. If you are struggling for content be brief, be sincere and round it off with a quotation on marriage. Everyone will remember the last thing you say, so finish with a flourish.

◄ Remember that anyone giving a speech at a wedding is talking to a friendly crowd which is willing him or her to do well.

The guests

One of the most frequent disagreements is who to invite and who to leave out, and considering that the reception is where most of the money disappears, it is also where you may need to prune your list.

It is not unknown for parents paying the bill to feel they can edit the guest list or include distant members of the family and long-time friends, some of whom mean little to the bride or groom. This can cause annoyance to a couple who may be reluctant to leave out old work colleagues or feel squeezed to ask friends to come without partners, just to make room for people their parents feel have to come 'because we went to their daughter's wedding'. You can try – although it won't always succeed – to work out the number of people you really must invite and ask the groom's family to do the same. If you tell someone they can invite 50 people regardless, they will find 50, even if – in truth – they only really want to invite 40. Don't end up with ten guests that mean very little to anyone.

◄ Consider splitting established groups. For instance, if your tables all seat ten people and you have twelve university friends, split them into two groups of six and mix them with work friends, rather than leave out just two to sit alone.

Seating plans

This can be as easy or complicated as you want to make it. All you can do, as hosts, is arrange your guests as best you can within the constraints of the space available. You cannot ensure that every table will be a buzzing, joyous hub of lightning wit and repartee. You also cannot ensure that everyone will know/like/get along with everyone else. All you can do is choose a good mix:

DO write down all the names, cut them out and spread the pieces around the floor, swapping them around to build up your groups. Arranging them around upturned saucers or plates to represent tables gives you an even better idea of your overall seating and shows you who will back onto whom.

DON'T ask friends 'would you prefer to sit with A or B?'. It's your choice, not theirs. Everyone will want to sit with the fun people and you may end up with singles and couples you can't place.

DO keep families, particularly the older generation, together during the meal. They can mingle later.

DON'T get bogged down with the boy-girl-boy-girl traditional seating. Not only does it make singles feel uncomfortable, but it can sometimes be almost impossible to get right and you end up splitting good friends just for the sake of convention. Put people together because of their personalities, not their gender.

DO try to keep young children together on tables where most guests are child-friendly and keep them away from doors where they can escape or catch their fingers. On no account put them near the table with the cake!

DON'T forget that on big tables, people only ever tend to talk to those either side of them, so in some ways it is more important to consider their next door neighbours than the overall mix.

▲ Don't fret too much about placing people who don't know each other together on a table. It is only the first few minutes where conversation can be forced. By pudding, everyone will be really enjoying themselves.

Things to watch

As your wedding party gets into full swing, most of your worries will take care of themselves, but there are a few things that you can consider in advance which will make everything run even more smoothly.

Brief your team

You will have more than enough to think about on the day without worrying over every little detail. This is not so much a must-do for the bride and groom, as a checklist for the couple to discuss with their best man, chief bridesmaid, master of ceremonies or venue manager before the event, so that someone has every angle covered.

Party pointers

All guests enjoy themselves in different ways. Some will be in a hurry to start the dancing, a few will want to chat over coffee indefinitely and others will be reluctant to drag themselves away from the bar. If the DJ is not due to start until 9 o'clock, for instance, but is all set up in anticipation and guests seem ready for some music, perhaps the DJ could begin a little early? Alternatively, if the disco really isn't going very well and guests are reluctant to throw themselves around the dance floor, a good DJ should be able to switch the playlist accordingly. If he doesn't, someone needs to be on his case.

Is there a private room where nursing mums, elderly or sick relatives can rest?
If you are in a hotel, this is usually easy to arrange. Either agree that the key be left at the reception desk, or have it held by the best man. Remember a room is for the use of the elderly and guests with young children – not for sullen teenagers to hide away in.

▼ Children do get tired, so friends with young families may have to leave before the end. Make a point of chatting with them all and making a fuss of the little ones early on, so that if they have to suddenly go, you don't feel guilty for ignoring them all day.

YOUR RECEPTION

▶ While it's important to ensure adequate supplies of alchohol, do not neglect those who may be abstaining or who simply want a break from the booze. Ask your venue manager about the possibility of a coffee/tea bar – basically a small table with a permanent pot of coffee and a few interesting flavoured Indian and fruit teas – from which guests can help themselves at any time.

Is that smoke I can smell?

People often start the day behaving themselves, but after a few drinks they forget where they are and begin to light up. If you have asked guests not to smoke, or if the venue prohibits it, someone has to play warden and make sure everyone goes to the designated areas for a cigarette.

How is the drink lasting?

Depending on how you have structured your party, you may reach a stage where the alcohol runs out – either because the cases of wine you ordered are finished, or the cash float you put behind the bar has run dry.

Make sure someone (your best man, maybe?) has the authority to sanction another fixed amount of drink behind the bar or order a

▲ If someone you know has a Polaroid camera, offer to pay for some films if he/she will take some random photos of guests during the day, to pass around in the evening or to stick up on a pin-board or seating plan as the party progresses. Discussing photos always gives people who don't know each other an opening line.

set number of additional bottles with the catering manager. He may agree to put any extras on his credit card – to save bothering you on the day – and ask you to settle up later. However, this can lead to an embarrassing moment six weeks later when he has to ask you for the difference.

Is it all too much for some?

Elderly relatives will often stick it out until the bitter end, even though they are tired, or because they are expecting lifts from other family members. It's a good idea to leave the best man with some cash for cabs, just in case someone prefers to slip off a little early.

Time for coffee?

Someone has to call a halt to proceedings and there's nothing worse than a party that stops unexpectedly. The lights suddenly go on and, boom, it's thank you and good night. Ask the best man to keep an eye on the clock and ask the kitchen/bar to serve some trays of coffee as a gentler way to indicate that the end is nigh.

Drunken guests

The sad truth about weddings is that you can't ply friends and family with alcohol all day and then be surprised when someone has one over the eight. This is where your choice of best man is really important. Arguments, fights, or people falling over and being ill are all by-products of too much booze and should be dealt with quickly and quietly.

If someone is seriously drunk, take their car keys from them and put them in a cab. The longer they hang around, the more their family is embarrassed by their behaviour. Not only that, but they become the star of the show and that's your job!

TOP TIP

No bride ever claims that her reception dragged. It is the fastest party on record. One minute you are taking your first sip of champagne, the next you are bidding everyone good night. Savour each moment and don't feel you have to have a full conversation with everyone.

want to know more?

Take it to the next level...

Go to...
▶ **Saving money** – page 60
▶ **Stationery** – page 88
▶ **Principal players** – page 54

Other sources
▶ **Websites**
  For help with writing speeches
  www.witty-wedding-speeches.co.uk
  www.crispandcheerful.co.uk
  www.wordsmith.org
  For help with choosing music for the
  ceremony and reception, including samples
  www.topweddingsites.com
  For booking music and entertainment
  www.alivenetwork.com

Setting

a style

However clear you are about your own outfit and the styles the groom and bridesmaids will adopt, a wedding is a mix of many different styles and tastes. Let guests know of any particular dress code if you have one – so there is some consistency in the photos – and then relax. Seeing what everyone has chosen to wear is part of the fun.

The tone of the day

You can't tell your guests what to wear, of course, but as they are going to feature heavily in your photos, it's better to share any fixed style ideas with everyone beforehand.

No-one wants to be the only guest wearing a hat (or without one), so it can help to let people know that your wedding is going to be either very relaxed or very formal. For years it was considered bad form to put a dress code on an invitation, but if you are hoping for a certain style, it is fine to add the line 'black tie' so that men know what sort of suit to hire (or break out of mothballs) and ladies know to wear evening dresses. Black tie has always been popular at Jewish weddings and is increasingly chosen for late afternoon weddings at a licensed venue where the ceremony can flow into the reception. Other dress themes, such as the groom asking his male guests to wear something in a certain tartan, can be discussed informally by phone or e-mail.

Time of year

Winter weddings tend not to be as colourful as spring and summer celebrations because people dress for warmth rather than style. As plain and dark shades tend to predominate among coats – for both men and women – consider using more black and white film for your outside group shots, rather than colour, which may not work so well with the prevailing beiges/greys and browns.

◀ For a summer wedding choose lightweight fabrics such as cotton and linen to stay cool. Forget the silk – although it's light in texture, it's an insulator and may make you feel uncomfortably warm.

Here comes the bride

The wonderful thing about getting married is the way everyone encourages you to go on self-indulgent shopping trips for what is possibly the most expensive and elaborate outfit of your life. Just be careful whose opinion you heed.

Choosing a dress

Who would you trust with your life, your deepest secret and your last Rolo? Ok, this is the one person to take with you on your dress-buying excursion. Resist the temptation to make it a coach party outing, as you will only end up confused and exasperated. Everyone has their own idea, usually based on what they would like to wear themselves or what they chose for their wedding. No matter how close you are to someone – even your mum – beware of well-meant advice. Adult bridesmaids may also (unwittingly) try to influence your decision, based on a pre-conceived vision of what they are going to wear. Do some initial trying-on alone, then ask your trusted friend when you have whittled the styles down to a few possibilities.

Different designs

The sort of service you will receive depends largely on the money in your bank and your love (or not) of shopping. If you are a standard size, you may be able to buy off-the-peg from a high street shop or department store. Many now do evening-style dresses which you can try on, pay for and take home that day. Job done. The next step is to try samples at one of the bridal chains. These offer a variety of designs in a variety of sizes (although the larger the size, the less chance they will carry samples in all styles). You basically try on the samples, matching them with accessories and shoes on display, and then you order the dress you like in your size.

FITTING ADVICE

Whoever you go with, listen to the experienced advice of the assistants. Obviously they want a sale and they are going to say you look lovely in lots of things, but they also help brides find the best fit every day. They know which fabrics crease the most, which shades work best with which skin and how to hide myriad figure flaws. If you are going for a made-to-measure style with an independent designer, their advice is equally valuable. You will be a walking advertisement for their label and they want you looking your absolute best.

Made-to-measure

This is the sort of service you can get by going to a smaller shop which sells a variety of designer names or by going directly to a designer. The designer still has his or her basic styles, but the dress is made to fit your particular size, i.e. you may be a standard 12 but with particularly narrow shoulders, so the designer's version of a 12 in your chosen style will be made specifically to your measurements. This doesn't mean you are getting a one-off design – it is still a standard pattern – but it is a bit more custom-made. Obviously this is more expensive than buying from the high street or a bridal manufacturer. Sometimes, if the designer has a style you like but you prefer the sleeves on another design, you can mix and match but you will have to pay for the extra labour in (pardon the pun) marrying the two designs together.

Unique designs

If you have a vision in your head of the exact dress you want, but cannot find it anywhere in a shop, a designer can bring that vision to life, but the price of a couture service is going to reflect the time spent developing the design, cutting the pattern and the labour and skill involved.

LISTEN TO THE PROFESSIONALS

Don't underestimate the importance of good underwear. A good designer or shop assistant will be able to advise you which style of bra would be best under a strapless, sleeveless or slashed-back dress. Unless your dress has built-in support, don't be tempted to go without a bra because you are worried about the straps showing. A good bra will give you a flattering shape, whereas a bosom that's flattened downwards by a fitted dress will be obvious in the photographs. If you are sure you can return the spares, buy a number of different styles of bra and take them to your dress fitting so you can work out which suits best.

The shape of things to come

Princess
A popular cut which suits most figure shapes.

A-line
A good choice for pear-shapes and big bottoms.

Empire line
Sexy style for a big bust and covers wide hips well.

Bias cut
Can be unforgiving on big brides if not cut correctly.

Column
Can play down a plump tummy or a thick waist.

Ballerina
Better for taller brides as this style can swamp petite frames.

Shades other than white or cream
- Ice-cool colours such as greys, blues and lilacs suit blonde and fair brides with blue or grey eyes best.
- Brides with pale skin should be careful of very pale whites, which can 'grey' their skin, or pale, mint greens, which can make them look ill.
- Champagne, peach and shades such as caramel and cappuccino suit black or olive skin and brunettes or redheads.

Tips to flatter any figure

Full bust: Minimize with a long bodice or a cowl neck. Don't try to hide it with a high neck – better to disguise it with lace detailing. Or put it proudly on display with a sexy plunge neck.

Wide shoulders: Break up with a V-neck or wide straps and avoid cap or puff sleeves. A strapless dress will draw attention to swimmer's shoulders, particularly with hair swept up.

Broad hips: Draw the eye away with a centre seam down the front of the skirt. A-line styles are good for pear-shaped figures, so are empire lines (think Jane Austen costume dramas). Be wary of bias-cut column dresses, which cling.

Big bottom: If you have a 'shelf' backside, avoid a bow or back-fastening tie, which will draw attention to it. Consider a light train from the top of the bodice or waist instead.

Thick waist: Conceal a wide waist with a boned corset, or distract attention from it with a decorative jacket that falls just below the waistline. Avoid fitted ballerina styles

Fat tummy: A column dress can conceal a fat tummy, or play down a pregnancy, by elongating the torso. Opt for skirts with a seam down the front rather than a flat skirt or bias cut.

Petite frame: Try not to cut the silhouette in half with a corset and skirt. Bias-cut and column dresses give the impression of height, whereas full puff-ball ballerina styles swamp a short bride.

▼ Fine detailing, such as lace or little buttons, can draw the eye away from figure flaws you would rather not advertise.

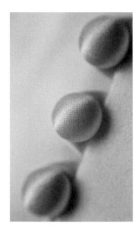

◀ If you don't fancy a traditional veil but would like something a little out of the ordinary, feathers have just enough va-va-voom to make you feel special without feeling over-dressed.

VEILS

• Veils should complement a dress, not swamp it. Veils tend to vary from just below the shoulder (the shortest style, which usually comes in two or more tiers to create height, often made from nylon net), through to waist-level or hip-level (a good length to show off sparkly edging, ribbon or detailing to match the dress), to full-length, train and finally cathedral. This, as the name suggests, is the veil you can visualize flowing along the cathedral/church aisle behind you.

• The longer, floaty veils tend to come in silk tulle. A full-skirted, ballerina's tutu-style gown works well with a shorter bouffant veil, while a bias-cut or column-style dress favours a long, sweeping train.

• Before you make any expensive purchases, consider how the veil will work with the hairstyle you have chosen and how you will attach it, i.e. using either combs or hairpins or by backcombing. How will the underpinning be hidden, i.e. under a tiara or headdress? Have a word with your hairstylist to see if your plan will actually work.

The groom

Never forget this wedding stars two people, so while the bride is disappearing under an avalanche of organza, the groom needs to decide exactly what kind of dash he would like to cut. The choices may not be as wide as for the bride, but for someone who, say, lives in jeans or wears a uniform for work, it can be just as bewildering.

Choosing a style

There are a number of styles a groom and his party (best man, ushers, fathers, brothers, close friends) can choose. If you choose a particularly unusual or rakish style, however, make it clear that not every male guest is required to follow it. Some elderly uncles or granddads simply won't feel at ease in velvet brocade or a Nehru collar, and the Mr Darcy look does not suit all sizes! The basic options are:

Lounge suit

A standard 2- or 3-piece tailored suit. Virtually any colour apart from black is acceptable (e.g. beige, brown; dark, medium or light grey; dark or navy blue; or even cream, sand and pastels), jazzed up with a flamboyant tie.

Morning wear

Top hat and tails. This dates back to the days when couples married in the morning (hence the ceremony was followed by a wedding 'breakfast') but doesn't apply so much now. You can have a 3pm wedding and ask your guests to come in morning wear without breaching any 'etiquette' rules. Morning wear traditionally comprises a black, grey or navy single-breasted tail coat, pinstripe trousers and a wing-collar shirt with a silk tie or cravat. Styles are now available to order in a box-cut rather than tail coat if grooms prefer. You don't actually wear the top hat, by the way, but carry it by the brim in your left hand.

Frock coats

Picture the Edwardian dandy and characters from Oscar Wilde plays or remember the Nehru-style collars from The Beatles' albums for the latest trend in 'occasion wear'. These styles can be a lot of fun and jackets can come in anything from burgundy velvet or brightly coloured silk, to cool cream or white. Obviously this is a dress style you will almost definitely have to hire, although some grooms like to have a jacket specially tailored, while his party and close family hire something complementary.

Highland wear

If there is Scottish blood in the family, you could go for something from the clan tartan, if you know what it is. This doesn't have to be a kilt, but can be plaid trousers or a plaid waistcoat instead. And you don't need a tartan specialist either, as many high street rental chains now carry a comprehensive range of Highland wear.

Black tie

Traditionally not worn until after 6pm, this is often a popular choice for guests as it makes men feel 'dressed up' rather than 'on display'. Many men also own a tuxedo already, so it is less of a sartorial departure than a silk brocade, Regency dandy jacket.

White tie

This is still considered very James Bond or ambassador's cocktail party, although if you want a very formal affair, this too can be good fun.

◀ It is nice to match some of the shades between the bride and groom, whether it is the groom's waistcoat and the bridesmaids' flowers or the bride's bouquet and the colour in his tartan. Beware of trying to theme everything, however, which can look forced.

Style to hire

As around three-quarters of weddings in the UK take place between April and October, most formalwear hire suppliers find that their busiest time for enquiries is between September and January, with the majority of bookings between January and May. However, to ensure your chosen range is available in all the sizes needed, make sure your order is in at least three months before the wedding date, especially in high summer. If the groom's party, family and ushers come from different parts of the country, choose a supplier with nationwide branches so that each person can actually go in and try on a suit, not just order it over the phone.

Most hire companies should be able to cater for everyone from a very big man right down to a small boy, but if you want a few non-standard sizes, make enquiries early as they may have to order them in from other branches.

Tailor-made

This is, of course, one time in a groom's life when he can splash out on a really smart, tailored or designer jacket or suit. Make sure the original measuring and fitting session is done in plenty of time, preferably with six months to go. Top menswear designers – like bridal wear designers – also get booked up well in advance and a made-to-measure suit takes time and many man-hours to craft. Be careful of ordering a style that is very cutting-edge and fashionable or, frankly, wacky. You will be looking at those wedding photos for many years to come and you don't both want to cringe every time you see the groom resplendent in his Rupert Bear check.

MUST KNOW

Fitting tips for guys

- **Tall and slim:** For beanpoles who feel swamped in a suit, try a fitted shape on the shoulder but not too much definition at the waist. Choose trousers with a fuller leg and consider a sturdy fabric, such as wool flannel, which gives body to a suit.
- **Short legs:** Consider a pinstripe and choose slim-fitting trousers.
- **Large-chested:** Bodybuilders often have a 'triangular look' because their shoulders are so wide, so go for an open-buttoned frock coat, which adds breadth to the midriff area.
- **Big men:** A double-breasted jacket can disguise someone carrying a few extra pounds, as can single-pleated trousers.

◀ Always make sure new shirts are washed once to lose that just-out-of-the-packet look and never choose a shirt with short sleeves or pockets, even if you think there is no chance of the jacket coming off at the reception. You never know how animated the dancing may become!

Co-ordination

Try not to lead your guests into some kind of theme. A rather woolly comment that 'we're all wearing grey' can be misleading because male guests may think they all have to wear a grey suit and you will have people arriving in a raft of shades from charcoal to near white and the group photos will look like a salesman's convention. Either be specific or say nothing. If the groom is in the armed services or in a uniformed profession, such as the fire service, it can really add to the sense of occasion if he and his work colleagues wear their dress uniforms (and finish the ceremony with a guard of honour), although make sure everyone is informed in plenty of time to get their dress uniforms cleaned.

When choosing formalwear:
- Always button the jacket on a morning suit.
- Shirts are usually white or neat stripes with a white collar.
- Shoes should be black, preferably lace-up, with black or grey silk or fine cotton socks.
- Wing-collared shirts generally go with cravats and standard collars go with ties. If you are wearing a stiff collar, take a spare. Avoid black ties as they are too funereal.

▼ Most menswear hire chains carry 'mini' lines for children, but you should never assume all lines will be available in all sizes all the time, particularly for the pre-school age group.

The bridesmaids

Whether they are worn by sweet little 5-year-olds or sexy 25-year-olds, the bridesmaids' clothes should complement rather than overpower the bride's outfit. And just remember (when you are trying to force redheads into burnt orange taffeta) that bridesmaids want to feel a bit special, too.

If your bridesmaids are different shapes – one tall and slim, the other short and cuddly – there is nothing to say that they have to wear identical dresses (as few designs suit every frame). It's the colour that will theme them most, so if you are having dresses made, choose the most flattering styles for each bridesmaid and just keep the colour consistent. If one girl has a heavy bosom, for instance, and another has a boyish figure, varied bodices and necklines might be needed. Avoid major differences however, such as one wearing long sleeves and another going sleeveless. Two-piece designs flatter most shapes and allow for some nipping and tucking. For bridesmaids who are self-conscious about a few extra pounds, remember:

● Slippery satin clings, is unforgiving and emphasizes every roll and bump.
● Shiny material catches the light and shows up 'padded' areas in the photos. Matt fabrics are more slimming.

MUST KNOW

Buying off-the-peg

If you have a selection of smaller bridesmaids of varying ages and want to buy ready-to-wear styles from the high street, watch your timing:

● Children have growth spurts and if you buy too early, you may have to let clothes out.
● However, don't leave purchases too late, especially in late summer (when many buyers consider the wedding season to be over and clear out stock until mid-autumn) or Christmas and New Year (when bridal floor space is often commandeered for seasonal stock and sale items).
● If you have, for example, a four-year-old, a seven-year-old and a ten-year-old, don't buy any outfits until you have tracked down the dress in all sizes. If you buy two sizes, then can't find the third, you will have to start again.
● When buying off-the-peg, the ten-years-plus age group is not well catered for, so a big nine-year-old may even struggle to find a fit. Look around with plenty of time to spare in case you need to have some styles made.

◀ Young bridesmaids love to feel like 'fairy princesses' but avoid the temptation to over-accessorize. When they are nervous or excited, little girls will unravel plaits, pick at lace trim and fiddle with flowers and bows. Simple styles, for example with bows at the back of the dress, often work best.

If you have bridesmaids that really can't agree on colours, you could always consider keeping the styles the same and varying the shades. If two look really good in light shades and the others favour stronger colours, mix and match by having, for example, two in peach and two in burnt orange, but make sure the tones complement each other, and redress the balance with flowers (i.e. the pale peach bridesmaids could carry burnt orange flowers and vice versa).

Who pays?

This, along with guest lists, is one of the most common causes for tears. It has become a trend for brides to ask adult bridesmaids to pay for – or at least contribute to – their dresses, the argument being that they would have the expense of an outfit anyway. However, they wouldn't necessarily be buying something floor-length and in lime green, so if they do agree to foot the bill, ask them not to buy a wedding gift to make up for it, or treat them to their hair and professional make-up on the day.

▶ Mothers dearest

The most important female cast members – after the bride and her bridesmaids – are the mothers. There aren't many 'rules' governing their outfits, but they are also centre stage for most of the day so they can afford to dress up.

The main restriction for the mothers of the bride and groom is not to wear white and to go for cream only if the bride is in something unconventional, such as red or gold. Trouser suits are perfectly acceptable, providing they are not too tight. If you feel comfortable in trousers, try loose-fitting 'dressy' trousers matched with a long flowing jacket with slits in the side, which tend to feel a bit more glamorous for a special occasion than a shorter, tailored 'interview' suit.

◄ Don't feel awkward about asking your daughter to accompany you on your own shopping trip. She may be busy, time-hungry and wrapped up in her own outfit needs, but she will also be flattered that you want her advice.

Hats

- Avoid heavy brims with high-collared jackets as the face tends to disappear into the neck.
- Big hats suit low necklines and balance well with three-quarter length jackets or long dresses. Avoid them with short, boxy jackets or boleros.
- Summery prints and floaty materials often go better with feathered or netted headdresses than with heavy hats.
- Always try to keep the brim of the hat within the width of the shoulders to avoid looking top heavy.
- Choose a hat that lets the light through or a style that has a brim which turns outwards, so as not to cast shadows on the face.

Two outfits the same

The big worry for most mothers-of-the-bride is how to look individual. If guests are all coming from the same area, it is likely that the women of a certain generation are going to look for their outfits and hats in the same specialist stores. There is a danger that the bride's mother will arrive in an identical dress/suit or accessory as someone else. Make it known early which colours you are wearing and the shades chosen for the accessories. If you fancy lemon with navy bag and shoes, circulate news of your choice on the grapevine early, so other mums, aunts and guests can steer clear of these colours.

No crying now

Be careful how you choose make-up for the wedding or you may have something else to cry about when you see the photos!

- Neutral eye shadows are easier to blend and open up the eyes.
- Dramatic, dark shades minimize eyes in photos.
- Shimmery eye shadows tend to accentuate fine lines, so choose matt.
- A little mascara goes a long way and can be reapplied after tears dry.

want to know more?

Take it to the next level...

Go to...
- ▶ Best man's duties – page 54
- ▶ On the day – page 164
- ▶ Suit hire return – page 174

Other sources
- ▶ Suit hire for the groom
  www.burtonmenswear.co.uk
  www.mossbros.com
  www.austinreed.co.uk
- ▶ Outfits for the mothers
  Big department stores such as Debenhams, Selfridges, House of Fraser; also mother-of-the bride specialists such as Condici (www.condici.com) and Jacques Vert (www.jacques-vert.co.uk)

countdown

It doesn't matter how many months you have to prepare, everything will seem to snowball as the weeks pass and the big day draws near. Just make sure that the final details, such as the ceremony rehearsal, hen night and honeymoon arrangements, are in safe hands (preferably yours). Then take a deep breath and stop panicking!

Compare diaries

So, you've planned your wedding within an inch of its life and the day is looming. Make sure you've communicated everything to the people who need to know.

Get out the diaries

The over-riding advice at this stage has to be 'assume nothing'. Has the groom made an appointment to have his hair cut in time for it to grow back a little, just the way you like it? You and the groom need to compare diaries and check the key dates and times. This is also when you need to chase any remaining guests who have neglected to reply to your invitations.

Who to ring and what to check

Officiant (registrar, vicar, priest, rabbi, etc.)

Has everything been booked, such as the bell ringers, choir, organist, etc.? Has anything cropped up, such as temporary traffic lights or road works, which may affect access to the ceremony?

Florist

Ask the florist to read out delivery addresses for the bouquets, buttonholes and corsages, ceremony flowers and reception flowers, including thank-you bouquets. Do they have a contact name and number for the ceremony/venue and has a suitable time been arranged for delivery? They could arrive at a hotel, for instance and find the reception room yet to be transformed and still serving breakfast!

TOP TIP

Ring, ring and ring again

Even if your trusty suppliers told you everything was arranged and they have banked your deposit, get in touch again a couple of weeks to a week before the wedding. Some may want payment in full, far enough in advance for your money to clear, to pay their suppliers or buy ingredients. Although it is unlikely that a reputable professional will refuse to supply you because the cheque hasn't cleared, don't take that risk. And double-check the basics – the date and time of your wedding. You may feel an idiot stating the obvious, but rather an idiot than a bride with no car or photographer!

Reception venue

You should have had most RSVPs by now so you can give your venue an idea of numbers. Check the latest time you can deliver a seating plan and ensure your contact knows who he/she is expecting, e.g. the cake will be delivered by so-and-so at such-and-such time.

Caterers

If your caterers are independent of the venue, check these two parties have already been communicating. It is a bit late now for the caterers to learn there are not enough ovens at your venue to prepare 150 soufflés! Now is the time to inform them of special requirements, such as vegan diets, or guests with lactose or glucose intolerance.

Cake suppliers

Check delivery address and contact name. If they are responsible for decorations, have they been able to get the exact flowers promised?

Entertainment/DJ

Check date and arrival time of DJ. Have musicians been able to track down any unusual music you requested in time to practice sufficiently?

Care hire company

Check your vehicle hasn't had any little prangs recently which required a paint job or a last-minute substitution. Check date, arrival and departure time, in case the photographer wants to get creative with a few car shots.

Menswear hire

Do they have all sizes ordered, especially for very large men or small boys? Confirm time of pick-up and when suits must be returned. Delegate the job of returning them while you are away.

Photographer/Videographer

Confirm date and time and suggest, if you haven't already done so, that you get together at the venue to discuss possible shots. Even better, see if they have time to come to the rehearsal.

Stationery

If orders of service still haven't turned up, chase them. These can be last-minute because religious ministers often want to approve them first, but a gentle reminder to the stationery company won't go amiss.

Looking good

Once you have chosen a photographer and decided on the photographic style, consider some tricks of the trade to add that final gloss. The right cosmetics, an understanding of shades that complement your colouring and a few rehearsed poses in front of the mirror can work marvels. Models and actresses don't look fabulous in those red carpet paparazzi shots by accident!

TOP TIP

- Never stand square to the camera as your shoulders are much wider than your head and you may look bulky. Turn about 30-40 degrees to narrow your profile and put one foot forward.
- If your dress is nipped in at the waist, don't hide it with your bouquet. This is the narrowest part of the torso and is best shown off.

◀ Practice pulling expressions in front of the mirror to work out if you have a best side and how you prefer to be captured on camera.

Keep it natural

Any stylist will warn you not to experiment with new make-up or dramatic hair styles on your wedding day. Instead, learn techniques that make the most of the way you look naturally – the look your soon-to-be husband fell in love with in the first place. Book a professional make-up artist if it will give you confidence, but have at least one practice trial. To glow in your photos, you are aiming for three basic things: a flawless complexion, wide-awake eyes and kissable lips.

Skin tones

Nothing can tone down an over-done fake tan and photos will only emphasize the orange glow, so be warned. Instead, opt for a light base or tinted moisturiser close to your natural skin tone so there is no obvious line between face and neck. Be sparing with blusher, too. You will glow with excitement naturally.

Eyes right

Emphasize eyes with a pale or neutral shadow on the lids, a darker shade across the socket for definition and a medium tone swept up towards the outer edge of the brow. Colours to avoid (unless you know they work for you) are oranges and purples. Waterproof mascara is a must, obviously, but don't apply too many coats in the hope it will last, as lashes just clog.

Lip service

You'll spend much of the day kissing family and friends, so treat yourself to a good lipstick. Apply once with a lip brush, blot and apply again. Don't be tempted to outline lips with a darker colour, because after a while, the tell-tale line is all you will have left. Add a slick of gloss for shine.

MUST KNOW

Dos and Don'ts
- Do experiment with an eyebrow pencil as it adds expression. When shaping the arch, emphasize the brow just above the pupil.
- Don't over-do bronzing powders, and remove excess with gentle dabs of sticky tape. Wiping it spreads particles even further.
- Do choose a lip shade dark enough to show in the photos but not so dark that it drains your face of colour.

Glowing and toned

Most brides are spurred into some kind of exercise/beauty regime at the prospect of being the centre of attention and looking fabulous in their dream dress, but be warned. If you are embarking on any kind of weight loss programme, aim to reach your target a good couple of months before the big day. The biggest gripe dress designers have is of ever-shrinking brides who come for their final fitting and have simply lost too much weight. This is especially important to remember if you have a fitted, made-to-measure corset or bodice, as excessive weight loss is almost guaranteed to reduce the size of your bust, too. Remember, also, that many brides drop an extra couple of pounds in the week or so before a wedding due to excitement or stress. Try to concentrate on stretching and toning rather than fat-burning, cardio-vascular exercise in the last few weeks.

▲ Have a trial make-up before the big day if you are not a natural dab hand at foundation and shaders, but don't be steam-rollered into adopting a look that doesn't feel like you.

STRIKE A POSE

For a fluid silhouette, stand with one foot in front of the other, with your knees slightly bent, and put your weight on the back foot.

Keep moving
● Any form of
exercise is ultimately
going to help you
sleep better, so try
not to view it as a
chore, but a good
way of minimizing
shadows, bags and
a tired complexion.
Keeping active will
also maintain your
metabolism and help
you process and
dispel toxins, and
keep trim and toned.

Arms and shoulders

One area many brides fret about is the arms,
especially as a high proportion of bridal gowns
are strapless or held up with delicate spaghetti
straps. Even the slimmest of physiques can
suffer from the unattractive 'chicken wing'
underarm effect.

If you have the time and inclination, a tailor
made programme of resistance weights
(including machines such as the pec-deck,
tricep and bicep curl and lateral pulldown) can
improve things in as little as eight weeks. Ask a
member of staff at your local gym for a
personalized programme and try to go three
times a week, not on consecutive days.

Failing this, devise your own programme
using two bottles of water or tins of beans.
Simply stand with feet shoulder-width apart, with
arms straight out in front and holding the
'weights' from underneath. Slowly lift alternate
arms to your shoulders and down again. Try ten
on each arm, then hold weights beside your
thighs and lift to a horizontal line, keeping
elbows tight to the waist and slowly release.
Repeat and relax. If your muscles ache the day
after the first few times you try this, you'll know
it's working.

Skin perfect

Revealing dresses also require a glowing back
and shoulders, so it is worth investing in a few
treatments, such as back massages (great for
circulation and lymphatic drainage), saunas (to
steam out those imperfections) or marine
mineral wraps (great for tightening skin and
helping reduce fluid retention and cellulite). All of
these, plus any form of stretching exercise such
as Pilates or yoga, will also bring some colour to
your cheeks and help reduce tensions and
muscle tightness.

The rehearsal

It may feel strange, or even unlucky, to run through the most significant and exciting day of your life like a panto rehearsal, but there are plenty of practical and emotional reasons why this is a couple of hours very well spent.

Why do we need one?

Unless you are a serial bride or wedding stalker, you are unlikely to know exactly what happens, which is why a run-through a week or so beforehand can clarify things in your mind. For a church ceremony, it is the chance to practise the walk down the aisle (dad can come if he wants, although providing the bride knows what she is doing, she can practise walking in with a bridesmaid). This may sound as if it is over-complicating something which is very simple, but if you are following the minister to the front of the church, you need to consider how far you let the minister get up the aisle before you start your approach. (This is less to do with ecclesiastical etiquette and more to do with letting everyone get a good look at your flowers and dress.) The same goes for the bridesmaids. There is no need to go up the aisle as a tight-knit bunch.

Reciting the vows

Many officials will ask if you would like to recite the vows during the rehearsal. If you feel this will be unlucky, you are within your rights to refuse. However, speaking these words in full for the first time can be a very emotional experience. If you are going to dry-up, tremble or cry, it might be better to do it now, rather than on the day. For church services you will also be shown where to stand, when to kneel and when to face each other.

MUST KNOW

Take your time...
Time the music you have chosen for your recessional (the music you walk out to), then time how long it takes you to turn from the front and walk back to the entrance of the church or venue. Many brides make a dash for the door in their excitement and end up not enjoying their special music.

Who should attend?

- The minimum cast should usually be the bride, groom, best man, chief bridesmaid/matron of honour and chief usher. Advised attendees are also any bridesmaids/pageboys aged five and over, ring bearers, whoever is escorting the bride or giving her away and anyone doing a reading or performing a musical solo.

- Those not playing a significant role should stay away, even mothers of the bride and groom or siblings if they are not reading, performing or acting as ushers or bridesmaids. Generally, the more people you have, the more divided opinion follows.

- You don't need all the ushers, just the head usher. That's why you have one. He or she can then decide how to divide up the tasks and plan who stands where. If everyone attends the rehearsal, individuals tend to decide what they would prefer to do, rather than focus on what will lead to the most smooth-running ceremony.

- Weigh up the wisdom of asking small pages or bridesmaids. Under fives tend not to listen to instruction or remember much, and on the down-side they may take one look at the intimidating empty hall or church, take fright and refuse to play the game on the day. Often they are better thrown in at the deep end, particularly if they can follow older attendants.

Speakers and performers

If you are hiring a professional trumpet soloist or harpist, they should know what they are doing and should not be required to attend your rehearsal. In fact they would almost certainly charge you extra if you did ask them. However, if a friend or family member has offered to play some music, it is an idea to bring them along so that they – and the official or minister – can establish the acoustics and positioning. Anyone who is giving a reading is advised to come too, as they need to know where to stand, where to put the reading (i.e. will they hold it or is there a lectern?) and whether they need amplification. (Most readers will be excited enough to remember to bring their poem or bible reading with them, but put a spare copy in your bag just in case.) Remember the church or hall will be empty so the sound will carry differently to the wedding when it will be packed with people, although an experienced official or minister will take this into account. The rehearsal is also an opportunity for the couple to invite the minister to the reception or to privately thank their attendants and present them with a gift. Come the big day there is often too much going on.

Stags and hens

For committed party animals, the stag or hen night is the first thing that springs to mind when a couple announce their engagement. However, it is often one of those things that gets left late in the organization stakes, although, carefully monitored, it can be left to trusted friends.

Stag and hen parties are traditionally supposed to represent the couple's last night of independent freedom, but it is a brave hen or stag who actually plans their swansong as a single the actual night before the wedding. Invariably there is alcohol involved and unless you are going for a quiet meal with a couple of friends (and few brides or grooms are allowed to get away with that), a decent recovery period is required.

Who arranges it?

Traditionally the groom's party was arranged by the best man and the bride's by her chief bridesmaid or best friend. However, as the average age of marrying couples has crept up, so the emphasis for these occasions has shifted from the traditional raucous night at the pub or a club to more adventurous, lengthier (and costlier) weekends. When this amount of time and money is required, the decisions of where, when and for how long to go need to be taken more multi-laterally. It is not feasible for a bride or her matron of honour to announce the hen weekend is at an upmarket health farm or in a foreign country and expect everyone to part with several hundred pounds without prior consultation.

Who pays for it?

This is a tricky point. Unless the bride or groom is extremely rich, or generous or both, guests at each party are usually expected to pay for themselves. In the more traditional pub crawl guise, this meant everyone took their turn at buying a round or contributed to a whip. Equally, if the hen night is in a local restaurant and everyone has a good idea of how much the divided bill will come to, they can budget accordingly. However, if the bride or groom fancies something a little more unusual, there may have to be a compromise. Friends often don't mind paying a little more, providing they have an idea of what may be involved. Alternatively, if the plan is a little ambitious, it is an idea for the bride/groom to contribute so much herself/himself and ask for the balance to be borne by the guests.

▲ Hen nights can be healthy and holistic or crazy and carefree. The secret is to tailor the event to the bride – not the crowd – and choose something that she can look back on and remember – not regret!

Suggestions for her:

Spa days

Many health farms and spas offer one-day deals which include pools, Jacuzzi, steam and sauna and sometimes a gym. Treatments and massages might cost extra, but if there are a lot of you, there will be so much opportunity for gossip and giggling, you may not need them.
Bride might pay: for lunch with wine.
Guests might pay: for their own daily ticket and treatments.

A day at the races

A great excuse to get dressed up and have a flutter. There is usually a horse with a love-related name. Hire a minibus to take you, wait and return, and pack some coolers with fizz or wine and ready-made sandwiches.
Bride might pay: for transport and picnic.
Guests might pay: for course ticket and wine.

A night away at a hotel

Most chains welcome large groups of women, although it may be better not to use the word 'hen' when booking. Target hotels that are frequently used by business people, which tend to empty at the weekend, and see what deals they can offer for three or four sharing. You may be surprised. Hotels would rather earn a low rate than have rooms stand empty and they bank on you putting a fair amount across the bar.

Bride might pay: for drinks and wine.
Guests might pay: for equal share of room costs and dinner.

A meal in

Rather than invite everyone out to dinner where you can't always monitor the spiralling costs of what everyone orders, invite friends to your home instead. Either order a generous takeaway or ask a local restaurant if they will prepare and deliver a two- or three-course meal, depending on space available. Then rent a classic girly film, such as *When Harry Met Sally*, or wheel out the karaoke machine.

Bride might pay: for the food and film.
Guests might pay: for a bottle of wine each.

MUST KNOW

Who to invite?

If you are someone with a lot of friends from many different facets of your life, it is not always workable to invite everyone to everything. The danger here is that you worry all evening about whether someone from work is being left out or whether your younger friends are getting a bit loud for your aunties and you don't actually enjoy yourself. Get round this problem by having a series of mini nights out instead. Suggestions include:

● A lunch or after-work drink a couple of weeks before the event for all your work colleagues. If there are one or two special ones who are coming to the wedding, too, you can always have a quiet word with them about coming to the 'more official' hen night separately.

● A family lunch or supper which includes the mothers and more sedate relatives who would not relish dancing on tables in a wine bar but nonetheless would like to mark the occasion with a drink or a meal.

Suggestions for him:

Tickets to a sporting event

If the groom has friends with a shared interest in sport, tickets to a cricket match or motor race is a novel idea. If the tickets are costly, and the sport is mainly the groom's passion rather than his friends, the groom could suggest subsidising the tickets to make them more affordable.

Groom might pay: for some/all of ticket costs.
Guests might pay: for lunch and drinks.

A weekend camping or caravanning

This can be a real laugh and is much cheaper than a hotel. Obviously, it helps if there is a golf course or archery, paintballing, etc. nearby.

Groom might pay: for golf or other activity.
Guests might pay: for equal share of camp site costs and drinks/food.

An SAS training day

Various events companies offer military exercise days, which are always good for breaking the ice if the guys from work don't know the lads from the football club, etc.

Groom might pay: for a contribution to the events plus spoof prizes.
Guests might pay: for the balance of events costs plus drinks.

A quiz night

The cheapest option of the four but it involves the most planning. Hire a room above a pub, get some props such as buzzers, prizes, pads and pens, and organize your own quiz. You can buy books on most subjects, from music and film to politics or sport, from any big bookseller.

Groom might pay: for room hire and props.
Guests might pay: for drinks.

▼ There's nothing like a Boy's Own adventure day or a sporting activity to bring out the competitive streak, and it offers great anecdotes to work into the speeches.

The honeymoon

The guests have drained their glasses and your budget, but hopefully you have put a little cash aside for a honeymoon. Your first holiday as husband and wife should be a memorable one.

In a famous episode of *Friends,* Monica and Chandler attempt to milk their newly married status for honeymoon extras and treats. Like many honeymooners, their fictional characters were attempting to appeal to tour operators' more romantic side and it is worth a try. Even when you book, make sure the travel agent knows it is a honeymoon, as there is often an automatic room upgrade or welcome fruit/champagne/chocolates in your suite. The odd airline may recognize honeymooners with a complimentary bottle of champagne or a cake, but it is unlikely you will receive an upgrade on your seats to first or business class. It is worth asking, of course, because it is not unknown for couples to be moved forward in the plane.

MUST KNOW

Insurance

• If you are travelling with your maiden name on your old passport, check whether any travel insurance needs to be consistent with this or whether you can use your new married name if you prefer.

• Don't skimp on medical cover, especially when travelling in the US, and ensure you have repatriation provision in case you need to be flown home for medical reasons.

• If you are having a go at something daring and dangerous, such as white water rafting or ballooning, check what is and isn't covered before you take the plunge.

Check the currency

As your preparations snowball, it's easy to overlook ordering foreign currency or travellers cheques. Think ahead because it could save you money. Investigate which currency and method (US or sterling traveller's cheques or cash) is best for your destination. For some places, you are not actually allowed to take in any local currency. In Sri Lanka, for instance, you can only get Sri Lankan Rupees once inside the country. You need to carry a currency, such as US dollars, which is universally accepted. Once you break into your dollar bills on arrival, you'll have change in local currency, which you can use as tips.

Passport names

As a newly married woman, you can still travel on your old passport. However, it is vital that the name on your passport is the same as the name on your travel documents (flight tickets, hotel reservations, etc.), so don't be tempted to book tickets as Mrs Perry and travel as Miss Howes. If in doubt, pack the marriage certificate.

▲ Your honeymoon is a time to relax, so try not to pick over things that might not have gone according to plan.

want to know more?

Take it to the next level...

Go to...

▶ **Principal players** – page 54
▶ **Catering and cakes** – pages 66–75
▶ **Keeping on schedule** – page 116

Other sources
▶ **Websites**
For up-to-date road information
www.rac.co.uk/routeplanner
www.theaa.com
For rail information and timetables
www.nationalrail.co.uk
For flight information and timetables
www.baa.co.uk
For ferry information and timetables
www.ferryinformationservice.co.uk

On

the day

When the big day finally arrives, you will inevitably feel a mixture of excitement and anticipation…you have come so far now there is very little left to do but enjoy. Apart from running through a few last-minute checklists, the duty of any bride now is simply to look stunning and feel fabulous.

▶ # The big day arrives

Custom dictates that the bride and groom wake up at different houses on the big day and although some co-habiting couples feel this is a bit superstitious, most tend to follow the pattern. Just because they don't share the same roof, however, does not mean the bride and groom don't share the same excitement and panic...

Eat something

Your mother always stressed the importance of breakfast and you'd do well to remember her words today (that is, if she isn't already standing over you, force-feeding you porridge or toast!). Eat breakfast despite your nerves, because food will actually settle butterflies. You can't run a car without fuel and your body is far more complex than a motor, so try to think ahead. It may be many nervous, emotional hours and a couple of drinks before you see food again.

Fruit will help level blood sugar levels while cereals offer a good source of energy, but be wary of croissants and elaborate treats from the *patisserie* which may give you an initial sugar rush, then leave you drained after the boost subsides. Be wary too of excited friends who bring you a champagne breakfast of scrambled eggs with smoked salmon or kedgeree. If that's not the usual way you start your day, it may not be the best time to experiment with rich breakfasts. And go very easy on the champagne if it is still early, as alcohol can make nervous brides tearful.

Who's there?

Surround yourselves with enough people to keep you amused, sane and on schedule, but not so many that your wedding morning turns into a Marx Brothers film. Your guests will also

TOP TIP

In case you wake up with puffy eyes, pre-prepare some camomile tea and leave it overnight in ice cube trays. Then gently dab around the eyes. Professional models swear by it. Plain ice cubes will also work if you don't have camomile tea.

want to get themselves ready, especially your mother, and you might find yourself waiting for everyone else to get out of the bathroom.

If you have a lot of bridesmaids, maybe you could suggest that they should all get changed somewhere else – especially the little ones – and only rendezvous with you as the deadline approaches. (This is another very good reason to have a full dress run-through beforehand, so there are no horrid surprises on the day.) It is especially important to keep the numbers down if your photographer is coming to the house to take some moody, getting-ready shots.

▲ The morning of the wedding is not the time to discover that you all clash. Have a dress run-through a few days before and take outfits out of any protective plastic to let them air.

The art of delegation

There are always things that need to be done on the day and maybe some long-lost cousin will ring looking for a lift from the station or to ask where they can pick up their buttonhole, but it is important to keep things in perspective. What you haven't done by now isn't likely to get done in the time left, so work around it instead.

To do lists

If you are very organised, nerves can kick in quite early on the big day, so it is a good idea to have a few distraction tactics ready such as last-minute To Do lists.

Bride

- Ring your man and tell him that you are thinking of him.
- Put yourself first. Only one slice of bacon left? It's yours, honey, you're the bride!
- Have a long soak in the bath with oils to complement your fragrance (make sure it's not the first time you've used them though, in case of a reaction). Don't make the water too hot, either, or you may get blotches.
- Have your hair arranged in plenty of time. Ideally you should do your make-up last, just before you step into your dress, otherwise blow-drying or straightening irons may make your skin flush pink under all that carefully-applied foundation and blusher.

Groom

- Ring your fiancée and tell her you love her.
- Have the shave of your life. Maybe treat yourself to a professional barber? (You can be sure the bride is not skimping on her grooming!)
- Lay out shirt, tie, socks, cufflinks, shoes early, just in case something has been overlooked.
- Make sure the best man has all the necessary cash and paperwork to settle any outstanding payments with the church, registrar or reception venue, including tips.
- Whose car are you taking to the ceremony? Make sure the interior will stand up to the scrutiny of a photographer's camera. Chuck all crisp bags, football kits and old newspapers out. Obviously the car should have been through a car wash recently.

MUST KNOW

Brides usually go one of two ways. They either feel wobbly at the start of the day and then mellow out as their 'look' comes together, or they start out okay, then go rapidly downhill. Nerves at home are good, because it gets them out of the way before the ceremony. Once the adrenaline kicks in, nerves often disappear.

Bride's mother

● Look out for the flowers. The bouquets should be delivered to the house where the bride is getting ready. If the buttonholes are going to this address, someone needs to get them to the groom's party and/or the ceremony.

● Take responsibility for the bride's handbag, with things like brush, fragrance, make-up, mobile, etc. If the chief bridesmaid is carrying a little handbag or purse, the bride's lipstick, a comb and a few tissues could go in there.

● If some or all of the bridesmaids are getting ready at another location, the bride's mum can liaise with them in terms of any queries.

Best man

● Put a few spare direction sheets in your car for guests from out-of-town who may still get lost between the ceremony and the reception venue. If you are ordering any cabs to pick up from the ceremony, check they are still coming.

● Call a motoring agency such as the RAC or AA or go online to check potential traffic problems.

● How are you getting home after the couple go off? This is often overlooked.

● Keep your mobile on so that you can be the main point of contact for guests and suppliers, but switch it to mute during the ceremony.

● Check you have those rings and your speech!

Chief bridesmaid

● As the person the bride relies on most, the chief bridesmaid is there to help with the bride's hair, make-up, dress, jewellery and intricate underwear to go under skimpy dresses.

● The bride must remember that she asked this special person (sister, best friend) to have a supporting role in the main action, so at some point she has to let the chief bridesmaid get her own dress, hair and make-up organized.

MUST KNOW

PLEASE put someone in charge of doorkeys. Many newly wedded couples – or their proud parents – have got to the end of a fabulous night to realize that no-one has the keys to the home that the main players left from earlier that day. Or it dawns on them that the groom has them in his pocket – and he is now at the airport!

ON THE DAY

◄ As your ushers hand out the buttonholes, ask them to remind guests that they must switch off their mobile phones.

Arriving at the ceremony

Obviously the ushers need to be early, to check that orders of service and/or hymnbooks are available, if necessary, or that seating has been arranged as ordered for a civil ceremony. If the venue has only set out 100 chairs for 120 guests, for instance, now is the time to find out. The groom and best man also traditionally arrive early to greet guests. As guests arrive, try to monitor how the venue is filling up. If everyone is sitting modestly at the back, get them to all move forward to fill up the gaps. Now is the time to spread the word on confetti restrictions. Many venues do not allow it on the premises or within a distance where it can blow back inside. You may be safer with biodegradable petals.

TOP TIP

It has always been considered good luck to pay the registrar or religious official with an odd amount of money and many grooms choose to add a penny to the final amount to keep this tradition.

Keeping things in perspective

● Don't start worrying about the cost of little things now. If someone you invited mistakenly brings their partner because they thought she was included, smile nicely, ask the venue manager to pull up an extra chair and mentally add one person to the meal cost.

● So maybe the starter doesn't look exactly like the one you sampled at your tasting. Maybe the prawns are smaller, the garnish is missing or the peppers are a different colour. So what? The only person who knows about it is you, so tuck in and enjoy rather than tell all your guests 'it's not what we ordered'. You can take up any discrepancies with the hotel staff later.

● Most people are not going to mark you on your performance as a bride or judge you on your hospitality. They are going to be far too busy enjoying themselves to pick holes, and if they do, ask yourself why they are still your friends.

After the ceremony

If transport is provided, it is the best man and ushers' job to organize guests into buses or taxis. If not, it helps if they can establish who has a spare seat in their car to offer lifts to people without transport.

▶ Before all the cars drive away from the ceremony venue, ask the ushers to look under all the seats/ pews for camera cases, umbrellas or other bits and bobs that guests may have forgotten.

First night plans

Once upon a time, newlyweds cut the cake, threw the bouquet and sped straight to the railway station or airport to begin their honeymoon at once. Some barely made it to the end of their own reception before the taxi arrived. Today, few couples want to miss the end of their big party and elect to stay either at the location of the reception itself, or another special first night venue.

Obviously you will need overnight bags and someone needs to take responsibility for their transportation to the reception venue and make sure they are unloaded at that venue (more than one couple has got to the end of the party to discover that their overnight bags went home earlier in the boot of someone's car). In the confusion of the morning, the bride and groom often both forget to pack some door keys and then cannot get in the next day. This is a particular panic if they are due off on honeymoon, so give a spare set of keys to someone sober and sensible.

▼ Most brides choose to stay in their dress all day, although they often change into something slinky for the evening. If so, make sure someone is on hand to hang up that fabulous bridal gown in a secure room.

Your reception will flash by in no time and you may feel that the day is finished with you before you are finished with it! Don't get bogged down with things you feel you *ought* to do. Spend the evening with people you love, enjoying yourself, and leave the formalities until later.

• If you don't get to dance with everyone, at least make sure you dance with your dad or your husband's dad – and your new husband, of course.

• You don't need to have a debrief with the venue manager or the catering people about what went well (or didn't). This is feedback they can pick up later. And you don't have to go round thanking all the staff. It is their job and they are happy if you are happy. If they really impressed you, make a mental note to send them a thank-you card after the honeymoon.

• Don't spend the final hour of goodbyes apologizing for not being able to chat to everyone for long. Most people don't mind (or remember).

At the reception

Even if you have arranged for a gift list through a specialist company or a department store, some guests inevitably choose their own personal gift and bring it on the day. Don't attempt to open these and thank people on the spot. Ask for a table to be set aside, in full view of everyone (not tucked away where things could go missing), and direct guests to leave gifts there. If they offer you envelopes of money or vouchers, ask the best man or your father to tuck them away in their inside pocket until a later date, or check if the hotel has a safe box. Guests will inevitably press cards and little mementoes on you, which can be hard to keep track of. Try to store everything together in a couple of big bags or ask the venue manager if they have a box.

Coping with nerves

Everyone may be looking at YOU, but that's all part of the deal of being a bride. The key moments when you are under most scrutiny are: your arrival at the ceremony, the vows, the photos, the cake cutting and the speeches.

The arrival If, when you arrive at the ceremony, you are required to walk between assembled guests (which is usual), you have three options. You can stare straight ahead at the distant official, the altar, the wall or the window and therefore not catch anyone's eye. However, this will only underline your nerves and can make you look cold. Alternatively, you can lock eyes with your husband-to-be or a close friend and ask them in advance to return a steady stare, so that you can focus your breathing. This can still make you appear a little robotic. Or you can look from side to side quite quickly, catching people's eyes and then moving away, which helps avoid the frozen smile. This way also makes guests feel instantly involved.

The vows Hopefully you will be concentrating so much on what you are saying that you will be oblivious to anyone else. Try not to look around at guests at this point as their encouraging nods and smiles may distract you. This is the moment to fix your fiancé with a stare that shows you mean business. Don't worry about whether you will cry at this point. If you do get emotional, pause, take a deep breath and move on. If you

---

MUST KNOW

Beware the stiff drink

Some well-meaning friends may suggest you have a strong drink to steady your nerves before the ceremony. Only you know if this will be a help or a hindrance, but bear in mind that all your emotions are heightened today and if gin and tonic usually makes you cry, be sensible. One drink may help, more than that may make you unsteady or flushed.

are overcome, don't try to speak through your tears. Your minister or registrar will allow time for you to recover your composure. And don't be surprised If it's your groom who gets the lump in the throat. One minister confided that the men are always much worse (especially the ones full of bravado who joke at the rehearsal).

The photos This is the first chance avid fashion victims will have to get a good look at what everyone is wearing, so their attention may soon start to wane. Also, people will be chatting and saying hello, so you can afford to relax and enjoy the moment without worrying that a hundred pairs of eyes can see your bra strap.

Cutting the cake By the time you get to this stage, you will be an old hand at acting the star (and this is only a short scene anyway).

The speeches Most brides underestimate the impact of the speeches and the intensity of feelings towards them. All eyes will be on you again, especially when your father or new husband displays genuine sentiments, so have the tissues handy.

▲ Cutting the cake is a light-hearted event when you can afford to joke around a bit.

want to know more?

Take it to the next level...

Go to...
▶ **The role of the usher** – page 57
▶ **Bridesmaids' outfits** – page 140
▶ **Looking good** – page 148

Other sources
▶ **Last-minute material for speeches**
  Famous quotes on many subjects,
  including men, women, love, marriage
  www.aphids.com
  Famous events that happened on your
  wedding day
  www.entireearth.com
▶ **Check the weather**
  www.bbc.co.uk/weather
  www.metoffice.com

next?

So, it's all over. It happened. You're finally married and everything was wonderful. However, while you are both sunning yourselves somewhere fabulous, there are still tasks that certain friends can help you with. And when you return, there are still a few little niceties to be observed (plus a whole future to be explored).

► While you're away

While you're on your honeymoon – or even if you're just recovering from all the excitement quietly at home – there are all sorts of small jobs that willing friends and family can organize, so that you return revitalized, refreshed and reassured that everything is under control.

The wedding goes past in such a whirl that half the fun of the honeymoon is sitting on a beach or terrace somewhere, gradually recalling the events of the day. What you don't want hanging over you is a list of things that have to be sorted when you get back. You will probably have left deposits for anything hired and been given a time limit for their safe return. Chances are it is before you get back from holiday, so you may have to prevail on your willing chief bridesmaid, best man or mum just one more time.

Table, flower and cake extras

If you borrowed or hired vases, candlesticks, planters, lights, a cake board and knife or the little pillars that go between the tiers on a cake, these will also have to be returned within a deadline. Although most wedding suppliers appreciate that many couples go away immediately after the wedding, they have to set deadlines because another wedding may come along a week later needing the same equipment. Make sure you leave enough money with your volunteer to cover postage, taxis or petrol. They are already donating more of their time to help you, so it is only fair that you cover their expenses.

Menswear hire

The groom's outfit will probably be due back the first working day after the wedding. Generally speaking, the ushers and other male guests are responsible for taking back their own outfits, unless the best man feels particularly efficient and prefers to return the group booking altogether. Many hire companies will probably have charged a nominal fee to cover accidental damage within the hire cost, so this should take care of any run-of-the-mill marks or spillages, providing you haven't had an amateurish go at sponging them yourself. If someone has lost a top hat, however, they may find that this is not covered and they will be liable for its replacement. This is because many hire companies know from experience how easy it is to throw a top hat in the air and lose it!

Cleaning bridal gowns

Your bridal gown was probably the most expensive dress you ever bought and it saw one day's wear. If you have any sense, you'll have asked a friend or your mother to get it cleaned, even if its future is still undecided. Unless you plan to sell your dress or give it away, it needs to be treated and stored properly, and sooner rather than later.

▲ Dresses should be professionally cleaned as soon as possible. However, if your cream or ivory shoes have any stains on them, consider first whether you will want them dyed a darker colour before someone enthusiastically tries to get the marks out with chemicals.

Why the rush?

● The fresher the stain, the easier it is to get out, as all stains oxidize over time. Even if you cannot see those white wine spills on the morning after your wedding, by the time you get back from your honeymoon, the tell-tale rim marks will show.

● If possible, tell your volunteer what you think caused the stains – mud, chocolate, make-up, etc. – so that she can tell the cleaner and it can be treated accordingly.

● Never attempt to sponge stains yourself. When something is spilled on a fabric, the fibres swell to absorb the moisture. Once it has dried, a professional effectively has to re-swell the fibre before the stain can be removed. At least if the stain is undisturbed, the cleaner is only dealing with that alone. It doesn't help if the mark has been rubbed vigorously by someone armed with a tea towel, white wine vinegar and an old wive's tale.

SINGLE-USE CAMERAS

If you distributed single-use cameras for guests to use on the tables, ask whoever was responsible for collecting them to post them off for you as soon as possible. That way, you may have some snaps waiting on your return. If they are to be taken to a shop for developing, ask your volunteer not to collect them until you are back, so that you are the first to see them. Separate the negatives from the photos in case packets get lost while everyone is looking through.

▶ Now you are married

There is no legal requirement to change your name. The choice is yours (and your husband's) and you can continue to be known by your maiden name all your married life.

If you follow the traditional practice and adopt your husband's surname, presentation of your marriage certificate will be enough legal proof. However, most new brides are not actually prepared for the amount of bureaucracy this can involve, so get yourself organized with a list and prioritize who needs to know first because your new marriage certificate will be backwards and forwards in the post for some days, maybe even weeks. In all cases, invest in the additional expense of recorded delivery.

MUST KNOW

Name change checklist:
- Passport office
- Driver and Vehicle Licensing Authority (driving licence and vehicle registration document)
- Car insurance company
- Bank
- Building society
- Insurance companies (buildings and contents, health, extended warranties)
- Endowment pension or life assurance companies
- Employer
- Inland Revenue
- Union or professional association
- Utility companies (water, gas, electricity, phone)
- Mobile phone company (if on contract)
- Local authority (council tax and electoral roll)
- Doctor/dentist/optician
- Credit cards and store cards
- Mail order companies
- Share companies/investment broker
- Accountant/solicitor
- Premium Bond office
- TV licensing
- Internet service provider

▶ You will need your marriage licence to change your name on a number of documents. The obvious ones are the Passport Office and DVLA, but you may be surprised to find that the original certificate is sometimes required to change the name on a contract for things such as a mobile phone.

A quick phone call will not be enough to change the name on certain agreements or accounts and you will be required to send off your original marriage licence to many parties – for instance, when you change the name on your passport and your driving licence. Many financial and insurance companies with whom you hold endowment or life policies will also require either the original marriage certificate or a certified copy signed by a professional person, such as your solicitor or accountant. (Most organisations appreciate the hassle involved in changing your name and will return originals as soon as possible. To minimize the risk of loss, always post a letter containing your original marriage certificate by special or recorded delivery and enclose an SAE for its return.)

Double-barrelled names

Some women join their old name with their husband's – perhaps because there are no boys in the family and the name will disappear. This is best done by Deed Poll (documentary evidence that you have changed your name and that you are legally binding yourself to use that name – see 'want to know more', page 183). Some organisations may accept a marriage certificate as proof enough to change your records to a double-barrelled surname, but others will not so it makes life simpler to be prepared. If you register the double-barrelled surname after the wedding, you will each have to apply for a Deed Poll and pay twice. To save money, the groom can apply before the wedding, so that the double-barrelled name appears on the marriage certificate and the bride then takes the surname in the traditional way. Be careful of which names you change when, however, as it is a very bad idea to travel abroad with documents (i.e. passport or driving licence) showing different names.

Other name changes

If you decide against a double-barrelled surname but still want your original name to feature somewhere, you can keep the family link by turning your maiden name into your middle name. Again, this can be done by Deed Poll. If your husband chooses to take your name instead, he will have to do this by Deed Poll as there is not an automatic right to doing it this way as there is when a bride takes her husband's name.

Making a will

It's not a cheery thing to consider hot on the heels of a wedding, but a will is still very important, especially if one or both of you has children and the issue of guardianship comes into question or if there are children from former marriages and maintenance payment agreements. It is also a good idea to nominate your spouse as the beneficiary of any pension or policies in writing and, again, if children are involved, look into setting up trusts.

Married or living together – the differences

When it comes to property and inheritance, there are certain key differences between living together and being married.

● Unlike co-habiting couples, a surviving spouse will not be liable to pay inheritance tax on the assets he or she inherits.

● People who live together without being married are often not recognized by pension companies. However, spouses are entitled to inherit pension rights on the death of their husband or wife, although the terms of various pension companies and funds vary.

● Couples who live together cannot inherit from each other without a will. Married couples on

CHILD BENEFITS

If one or both of you has children, your marriage may affect the amount of Child Benefit you receive. The same is true of Child Tax Credits and you should inform the Inland Revenue of your change of circumstances in writing as soon as you return from your honeymoon.

the other hand can inherit without a will, although there are restrictions in the case of children. In this instance, the surviving spouse would inherit a given amount (in 2004 this was the first £125,000), personal possessions plus a life interest in the remainder; the rest would be divided between the children. This is the procedure if the partner dies intestate – that is, without a will. If there is a legal will, its contents and wishes overrule everything else.

Before you see a solicitor

Save time (and sometimes money) by addressing key issues before you seek legal advice.

- Work out the total value of your property, assets, savings, pensions, policies, shares and bank and building society accounts.
- Decide who is going to benefit from your will (your beneficiaries), both in terms of money and personal possessions.
- Decide who you want to nominate as guardians for your children.
- Decide who will be responsible for sorting out your estate and carrying out your wishes (your executor).
- One Plus One, the relationship research organisation, was set up 30 years ago to generate knowledge about couple and family relationships – how they work, why they run into difficulties and how to cope if they do. www.oneplus.one.org.uk.
- Other useful websites include www.advicenow.org.uk/livingtogether and www.adviceguide.org.uk. Advicenow.org.uk provides user-friendly information about the law and rights, with links to hundreds of web pages. It was launched in 2003 by Advice Services Alliance (ASA), the co-ordinating body for UK advice services.

▲ Marriage and partnership charity One Plus One offers an overview of the legal position of married and unmarried couples and parents. Go to www.oneplusone.org.uk and click 'married or not'.

▶ Lasting memories

Along with your wedding day memories, some things will live on forever, so take your time choosing beautiful photo albums, good storage boxes and elegant frames to show off your favourite pictures.

Once the dress is cleaned and the honeymoon tan begins to fade, you may think the excitement is over. Not at all – you still have THE PHOTOS. Most photographers will manage to get your proofs back in time for your return from the honeymoon and these come in a variety of formats. Some professionals are moving towards digital CDs, which literally offer a slide show of the shots which you can take to work and show colleagues or play at home. Others may offer the standard box of prints as a 'preview'. This is the more traditional method – although becoming less common – where the photographer offers a selection of numbered prints and the couple simply choose and keep the ones they want. This is a 'what you see is what you get' arrangement. A more flexible method is to view proofs, which show you the pictures as they were taken, but can be adjusted by zooming in, cropping or using techniques such as duo-tone and soft focus before they are finally printed.

Take your time over your selection and let a few people look at the proofs with you. If friends and family say they would like to have a photo to keep in a frame and leave the choice to you, pick different shots to the ones you are having yourselves. This way, every time you visit the friend or relative you will be pleasantly surprised and reminded of your wedding by seeing a photo you don't see every day.

▲ Some couples like to have special thank-you cards printed with their names and the date or even a small image from the wedding. You can choose any picture you like, from a family line up or smiling shot, to a close-up of a bridesmaid's bouquet or petals on a reception table.

Gift list delivery

Another big post-honeymoon treat is the delivery of your gift list items. It may sound obvious but try to arrange delivery at a time when you are both at home, alone, because the sheer thrill of unwrapping and unpacking all your gifts is a bit like being a child at Christmas and is something you need to experience together. Needless to say, if anything is incorrect or broken, get on to the gift list agent immediately, and be careful not to mention any mistake or damage to the generous donor.

Thanks so much

One of the things you cannot take too long over is sending thank-you cards. Although your guests appreciate that you have had a lot on your minds (and have probably been away), they may start to feel slighted if you have not acknowledged their gift six months later. This is not the occasion to buy a box of standard pre-prepared notelets and write 'To Bob and Carol, love Cathy and Ray' either. Try to write an individual note mentioning each specific gift.

Drying out

On the subject of petals, it's a nice idea to dry out any petals used as table decorations or scattered at the ceremony and then mount wedding pictures in large frames with the dried petals arranged around them as background. If you would like to dry and preserve your bouquet or a buttonhole, take advice from your florist first as some flowers are more successfully preserved than others. The simplest way is to hang the bouquet upside down in a dark place for a few weeks. Other types of flowers dry well if they are pressed against absorbent paper with heavy weights, such as a few big books. Covering the flowers in silica gel in a box lined with more gel is another method of absorbing their natural moisture, but again, ask your florist's advice. Whichever method you choose, your dried bouquet will hold together much better if you spray it with an acrylic spray to keep the petals in place. Or you could leave the task to the professionals and commission a flower-drying specialist, many of whom will be able to offer more creative ways of presenting and framing your bouquet.

ANNIVERSARIES

Tradition suggests that you celebrate your future anniversaries with a gift representing the following materials.

1 Paper	10 Tin	35 Coral
2 Cotton or straw	11 Steel	40 Ruby
3 Leather	12 Silk or linen	45 Sapphire
4 Books or flowers	13 Lace	50 Gold
5 Wood	14 Ivory	55 Emerald
6 Iron	15 Crystal	60 Diamond
7 Wool, copper or brass	20 China	70 Platinum
8 Bronze	25 Silver	
9 Pottery	30 Pearl	

Store your dress in pH-neutral (acid- and alkaline-free) tissue, ideally in an acid-free box. If you don't box it immediately, at least take it from the dry-cleaning wrapping, air it for a day, then cover with a white or cream duvet cover, tied at the top, and keep it in a dry, dark place. Don't risk keeping it in direct sunlight or covered in a coloured duvet cover, as some fabrics can absorb strong colours. Hanging a small pouch of lavender around the hook of the hanger can keep a stored dress smelling fresh.

What about my dress?

Brides traditionally kept their bridal gown to be made into a family christening gown, which is a good reason to get it cleaned and stored.

● If you want to try to sell it, do it straight away. The market for second-hand wedding dresses is limited, and you may have more success if it is a designer dress or in a large size, i.e. 18+. If it is a designer label, don't hang on to it too long as brides who really know about these things may not be so interested in last season's style.

● Be careful of trying to cut it down or dye it into a dress you can wear again. The reason you chose it in the first place was probably because it looked 'bridal'. Bridal gowns are also made up of so many varying weights of fabrics that dye is absorbed at a different rate and, frankly, it will be a bit obvious that it's dyed.

◄ It may seem over-the-top to make plans for what happens to things after the event, but when you have spent months choosing accessories, it's comforting to know your special shoes are safely stored away.

▶ Married Life

If anyone actually knew the format for a happy marriage, they would have patented it long ago and be living very comfortably off the profits. As newlyweds, all you can do is your best...your best at being a friend, a lover, a confidante and a life partner.

So you're married, congratulations. It probably all seems a bit new. You may still be fiddling a lot with your wedding band as you get used to wearing it and, if you changed your surname, there will probably be more than one occasion when you get a quizzical look from the supermarket cashier when your debit card says one name and you sign another altogether. At least you know how to introduce your man now. You can simply say 'this is my husband, Ray'. There's no more of that, 'this is my boyfriend, fiancé, partner, significant other...'.

▼ Married life is a learning curve for everyone involved and never more so than when children from previous relationships are involved. Whenever you feel unsure, remember – it's new for them, too!

If either of you has children from previous relationships, you will not only be working hard on your own new relationship as husband and wife, but also to build bridges and forge friendships with your partner's children. No-one who has done it will tell you that it is easy and if they do, they are looking through very rose-coloured spectacles. The sheer thrill of the wedding day – the champagne, the warm wishes, the flowers and the promises – can seem a long way away when a teenager slams a door in your face yet again, declaring 'you can't tell me what to do, you're not my mum/dad'. Hopefully, though, you knew what you were signing up for when you signed the register, and they do say a problem shared is a problem halved, so try to be supportive of each other, as with all things, and tackle the problem head-on, together.

The truth, as far as anyone who has been married a while will tell you, is that marriage has its ups and it has its downs and you will both have to compromise at times. There's an old saying that familiarity breeds contempt, but it doesn't have to and it shouldn't be the case if you truly love someone. However, over time familiarity can mean you begin to take each other for granted. So if, in a few years, you get to the end of a busy day and realize that you have not had a proper conversation, spontaneous cuddle or good night out together in ages, dust off those old wedding photos and lose yourself in a little romantic nostalgia for an hour. Then go and find your partner and tell them how much you still love them. It's what the big day was all about, after all!

▲ Hopefully your wedding was the fairytale day you dreamed about. Now it's up to you to make the Happy Ever After come true.

want to know more?

Take it to the next level...

Go to...
▶ Buying a home– page 16
▶ Joint finances – page 18

Other sources
▶ www.deedpollsonline.co.uk
   Deed Polls are not held at a central register but to enrol a Deed Poll (not a legal requirement) contact the Royal Courts of Justice on 020 7947 6000
▶ www.inlandrevenue.gov.uk
   Child Tax Credits and Child Benefit both come under the remit of the Inland Revenue. Leaflets are available on 0856 9000 404, saorderline.ir@gtnet.gov.uk or via PO Box 37, St Austell, Cornwall, PL25 5YN

Need to know more?

The list of resources and organizations that can help you is almost endless, but we hope these will at least point you in the right direction.

Civil ceremonies

British Humanist Association
020 7079 3580
www.humanism.org.uk

General Registrar Office, Northern Ireland
02890 252036
www.groni.gov.uk

General Registrar Office, Scotland
0131 334 0380

The Humanist Association in Scotland
0701 0704771
www.humanism.org.uk

Office of National Statistics
0151 471 4200
www.statistics.gov.uk

Registrar General for England and Wales
0151 471 4803

Registrar General for Guernsey
01481 725277

Superintendent Registrar for Jersey
01534 502335

Religious ceremonies

Baptist Union
01235 517700
www.baptist.org.uk

Catholic Enquiry Office
020 8458 3316
www.cms.org.uk

Church of England Faculty Office
020 7222 5381
www.facultyoffice.org.uk

Church of Scotland
0131 225 5722
www.churchofscotland.org.uk

General Synod of Church of England
020 7898 1000
www.cofe.anglican.org

Greek Archdiocese
020 7723 4787

Jewish Marriage Council
020 8203 6311
www.jmc-uk.org

Marriage Care (formerly
Catholic Marriage Advisory
Council)
020 7371 1341
www.marriagecare.org.uk

Methodist Church
020 7486 5502
www.methodist.org.uk

Office of the Chief Rabbi
020 8343 6314

Relate
0845 130 4016
www.relate.org.uk

Religious Society of Friends
020 7663 1000
www.quaker.org

United Reformed Church
020 7916 2020
www.urc.org.uk

Commonwealth bodies

Australian Government
Attorney-General
www.ag.gov.au

New Zealand Births, Marriages
and Deaths Dept
www.bdm.govt.nz

South African Dept of
Home Affairs
www.home-affairs.gov.za

Vows, readings & traditions

The Knot Guide to Wedding
Vows and Traditions
Carley Roney, Broadway Books.

The Nation's Favourite Love
Poems
Daisy Goodwin (ed.), BBC Books.

Wedding Vows and Traditions
Cathy Howes, MQ Publications.

Regional traditions & information

Ireland
www.ireland-information.com
www.irishweddingsonline.com

Scotland
www.house-of-tartan.scotland.net
www.scottish-master-of-wedding-
ceremonies.co.uk
www.siliconglen.com

Flowers

www.florists.uk.com
www.flowers24hours.co.uk
www.weddingflorist.co.uk

The Complete Book of
Wedding Flowers
Shirley Monckton, Cassell Illustrated.

Wedding Flowers
Paula Pryke, Jacqui Small.

Photography

British Institute of Professional Photography
01920 464011
www.bipp.com

Kodak Weddings
0800 783 7452
www.kodakweddings.co.uk

Master Photographers Association
01325 356555
www.mpauk.com

Professional Photographers Association of Northern Ireland
www.ppani.co.uk

Wedding Photographers online
www.findaweddingphotographer.co.uk

Directories of regional suppliers

www.confetti.co.uk
www.net-weddings.co.uk
www.weddingservices.demon.co.uk
www.wedseek.co.uk
www.weduk.com

Exhibitions

www.nationalweddingshow.co.uk
www.silverlinings.co.uk
www.theweddingguide.co.uk

Hen & stag nights

www.callofthewild.co.uk
www.hens.org
www.toptable.co.uk

The Alternative Hen and The Alternative Stag
Kirstie Rowson and Gemma Hayman, Virgin Books.

Entertainment

www.entsweb.co.uk
www.funtionjunction.co.uk
www.musicforlondon.com
www.theeventscompany.co.uk

Quotations & jokes

www.anyman.com
www.bestlovepoems.net
www.famous-quotes.com
www.lifeisajoke.com
www.quotationspage.com
www.yuni.com

Copyright

Books and journals
www.cla.co.uk

Performing Rights Society
www.prs.co.uk

The UK Copyright Service
www.copyrightservice.co.uk

Legal bodies

Deed poll services
www.change-your-name.com
www.oasis.gov.ie
www.ukdps.co.uk

UK Passport Service
0870 521 0410
www.ukpa.gov.uk

Index

Acknowledgements

● Contre Jour (www.orchidevents.co.uk): pages: 32, 37, 39, 51, 97, 98, 134, 175
● Corbis: pages 27, 53, 159
● Kerry Morgan (www.rethinkweddings.com): pages 1, 2, 3, 7, 8, 11, 14, 22, 42,
48, 56, 57, 59, 61, 62, 64, 68, 70, 71, 72, 74, 77, 79, 81, 83, 85, 86, 87, 89, 94,
101, 103, 105, 108, 111, 113, 115, 122, 123, 125, 126, 128, 130, 135, 139 (top),
141, 142, 148, 150, 163, 166, 167, 168, 171, 172, 181, 183
● Lucienne Sumner-Fergusson (www.bloomingfantastic.co.uk): page 78
● Suzanne Hodgson Photography (www.naturalweddings.net): pages 13, 21, 24,
35, 41, 55, 67, 92, 124, 137, 139 (bottom), 144, 160, 177, 179, 184, 185
● TopFoto (www.topfoto.co.uk): pages 28 (TopFoto/Chapman), 45
(TopFoto/ImageWorks), 47, 106 (TopFoto/Chapman), 121 (TopFoto/Chapman),
155 (TopFoto/Powell), 157 (TopFoto/ProSport)

C Collins need to know?

Look out for these recent titles in Collins' practical and accessible need to know? series.

Other titles in the series:

To order any of these titles, please telephone 0870 787 1732 quoting reference 263H. For further information about all Collins books, visit our website: www.collins.co.uk

Planning charts

A successful wedding – it's all in the planning...

▶ Wedding planner

Not every couple has the luxury of having twelve months to plan their big day. However, as so many weddings take place during high season (spring, summer and early autumn) and as popular venues get very booked up, our charts work on the premise that you will have around a year or so. We have broken key jobs down into three-monthly, monthly and weekly segments. These are the things we suggest you consider doing during this period to ensure that nothing is left to chance. Obviously, if you have less than a year to organize everything, condense the suggestions accordingly.

As soon as possible ☑

Informed friends and family of your intentions? . . . . ☐

Got both families together over a drink or a meal to become better acquainted? . . . ☐

Arranged any newspaper announcements? . . . . ☐

Agreed on type of ceremony you would like? Civil or religious, home or abroad? . . . ☐

Moving in together/buying house? Decided whether to do this before or after the wedding (as this will radically affect the budget)? . . . . ☐

Pencilled in some possible dates? Narrow them down. . . . . ☐

Checked availability of possible ceremony and reception venues? . . . . ☐

Set budget? Establish where the money is coming from! . . . . ☐

Taken out wedding insurance? . . . . ☐

Started looking around for an engagement ring? . . . . ☐

TOP TIP

Many a wedding dream has been spoiled because the happy couple 'assumed' family members would donate certain funds or 'assumed' they would be able to book their old family church or favourite golf course clubhouse for the reception. Remember the key wedding planning mantra: 'assume nothing'.

Twelve months and counting ☑

Checked ceremony availability and booked? Paid deposit? . . . . □

Checked reception venue availability and provisionally booked? . . . . □

Paid reception venue deposit? . . . . □

Arranged first meeting with the registrar or minister for your chosen ceremony?
Get a mini time schedule from them. . . . . □

Considered wedding style/theme? This may influence the time of day you
marry and party . . . . □

Started looking at bridal dresses to get an idea? Don't buy anything yet! . . . . □

Chosen principal players, such as best man and bridesmaids? . . . . □

Started putting a rough guest list together? Don't discuss with too many people
at this stage. . . . . □

Checked availability of key suppliers?
Florists. . . . . □
Photographers . . . . □
Videographers . . . . □
Caterers . . . . □
Cake . . . . □
Transport . . . . □
Entertainment . . . . □
Music . . . . □
Marquee . . . . □
Bar/champagne/wine. . . . . □

Considered hiring the services of a wedding co-ordinator if things are already
causing headaches? . . . . □

TOP TIP

Once you have decided with your fiancé who you would like as principal players (best man, readers, bridesmaids, witnesses, etc.), share the information with the people you have in mind and tell them the date. They may already have holidays booked or other immovable plans in the diary.

Nine months and counting ☑

Chosen honeymoon destination?. . . . . ☐

Paid deposit for honeymoon? If you don't do it now, the escalating costs will scare you and you may talk yourselves out of it later! . . . . ☐

Booked time off work for honeymoon and possibly a recovery day or two when you get back?. . . . . ☐

Passports in date? If they will have less then six months to run at the date of your wedding, consider ordering new ones . . . . ☐

Estimated catering costs (price per head for sit-down, fork buffet, finger buffet, etc.)? This will influence the number of guests. Even if you haven't yet picked the menu, make sure the caterers are booked and you have a rough idea of numbers . . . . ☐

Considered key suppliers, such as photographer, videographer, cars, DJ, master of ceremonies and musical soloists? . . . . ☐

Obtained quotes from key suppliers and made provisional bookings? . . . . ☐

Started narrowing down where you might order your outfit? Designers offering a made-to-measure service can get very booked up. . . . . ☐

Bought some bridal magazines and borrowed books from the library (for as much inspiration as possible)? Libraries usually have CDs and tapes of church and classical music you can borrow . . . . ☐

Started getting into the swing of any exercise, weight-loss or beauty regimes? . . . . ☐

Confirmed cast list (i.e. ushers, pages, etc.)? If people haven't been told, they may be assuming they are involved when they are not . . . . ☐

Informed guests if you are hoping for a no-children reception? Make sure everyone knows sooner rather than later. . . . . ☐

TOP TIP

Catering is probably the biggest controllable expense you will have. Ask for detailed estimates on possible menu combinations. A tweak here and a course dropped there can mean the difference between you being able to invite 80 or 100 guests, or mean that your friends from work can bring their partners after all.

Six months and counting ☑

Chosen stationery style, especially invitations? You will want them designed, proofed and printed in plenty of time to send out two to three months before the wedding day . . . . ☐

Ordered rings? If you are having them made, do it now . . . . ☐

Organized first dress fittings? Planned accessories? A certain veil or tiara, for instance, might mean you have to grow your hair a certain length . . . . ☐

Established dress code for the groom's party? Make the initial booking for any menswear hire . . . . ☐

Booked hairdresser and/or make-up artist for the wedding? Do it before someone else gets in and nabs your ideal time on the big day . . . . ☐

Chosen outfits for bridesmaids and attendants? Think ahead size-wise for growing children. Buy slightly on the big side and get the number of a good alterations tailor . . . . ☐

Remembered to hug your partner? Let them know how much you love them . . . . . . ☐

Ordered cake? Send the deposit if required . . . . ☐

Organized another meeting with your minister or registrar? Discussed finer points of readings, music and procedures? If you want bell ringers or a choir, now is the time to make sure they are booked . . . . ☐

Asked anyone to do a reading? Do they really want to? If they are a bit unsure because of nerves, you will need time to find a replacement . . . . ☐

Started looking at possible gift list companies? . . . . ☐

Arranged rehearsal date for the ceremony procedures? . . . . ☐

TOP TIP

Friends and family members will question you about gifts long before you have considered putting together a list, so it is as well to have some ideas in mind in advance. Many gift lists and gift registries only go 'live' a few weeks prior to the delivery date because of stock changes.

Three months and counting ☑

Established who is arranging the hen night/stag night, when it might be, how much it is likely to cost and who is likely to come? .... ☐

Cleared readings/music with minister/registrar so that any orders of service/ceremony can be ordered and printed? .... ☐

Started thinking about gifts for your best man, bridesmaids and anyone else who has helped enormously, such as the mothers? If they are to be personalized, engraved, etc. they need to be ordered in good time .... ☐

Booked first night hotel (if you are not staying at the same venue as the reception)? ☐

Checked budget? Assess what finishing touches you can afford, such as favours, balloons, table decorations, coffee and sandwiches at the end of the reception, extra entertainment, additional single-use cameras, etc. .... ☐

Finalized guest list? It will invariably change many times, but you need to have a master list for invitations .... ☐

Started pulling together any maps, B&B accommodation information and directions (by rail, by road) to go out with invitations? .... ☐

Sent invitations? .... ☐

Finalized menu? Any idea of proportion of vegetarians as yet? .... ☐

Arranged a wine tasting (so the venue can order sufficient crates of your chosen tipple)? .... ☐

Arranged another meeting with your florist? (Needs and tastes can change a lot from the initial consultation) .... ☐

Need injections for your honeymoon? Don't leave them too late .... ☐

TOP TIP

Get details of your ceremony content to your minister early, so that they can approve it in time for you to have orders of ceremony or service printed. Some will sit on them for longer than you have allowed in your time schedule and you may start to panic that the printing will not be done in time.

Two months and counting ☑

Organized a couple of chill-out days in a spa or health farm?. . . . . ☐

Looked around for a stylish guest's book and some blob-free pens or ink? . . . . ☐

Called all your suppliers just to double check details and dates? . . . . ☐

Booked final fitting for dress? Arrange a delivery/pick-up date. Be very careful
not to lose too much more weight . . . . ☐

Considered fake tan on the big day? Have a practice session now and see how
dark your skin might turn on the day and how quickly it will fade . . . . ☐

Booked a couple of manicures to experiment with acrylic tips? Your hands will be
on show a lot at your wedding and in the photos . . . . ☐

Arranged practice make-up and hair session? . . . . ☐

Bought any outstanding bridesmaids' dresses and shoes? . . . . ☐

Arranged collection of any hired outfits for the groom and his party? . . . . ☐

Do ushers know if there is a dress code and what is expected of them? . . . . ☐

Got to grips with the dreaded seating plan, even if it is only to let the venue know
what is expected of them? . . . . ☐

Will you want a top table, a cake table, a gift table or a temporary dance floor? . . . . ☐

Gently nudged guests who have not sent back their RSVP? . . . . ☐

Given details to everyone who needs to know about the rehearsal? . . . . ☐

Decided on who will draw up the seating plan? Will the venue prepare it in the
normal typed way, or do you fancy something a bit more unusual? . . . . ☐

TOP TIP

A venue will assume you want to follow their standard arrangements, i.e. top table in
one place, drinks table in another, unless you specify otherwise. Avoid the temptation
to break away from the norm without valid reasons. Things are often done a certain
way because of natural acoustics or dictated by natural light or spotlights.

One month and counting ☑

Chased final guests who have not sent back an RSVP?..................... ☐

Started on a rough seating plan? Think seriously about who to put with whom .... ☐

Bought honeymoon essentials? Do before wedding plans overtake everything .... ☐

Arranged lifts to and from airport?....................................... ☐

Ordered currency/travellers cheques? .... ☐

Got together with photographer to discuss possible shots? Better to meet
him/her at the venue and look for the best vantage points.................... ☐

Tracked down any outstanding accessories, such as flower girls' tights or
bridesmaids' hairslides?... ☐

Ordered single-use cameras? .... ☐

Attended final fitting for the dress? No more losing weight after this!............ ☐

Asked if guests can throw confetti or petals at the ceremony venue?........... ☐

Two weeks and counting ☑

Tried on your entire outfit (shoes, tiara, dress, jewellery and underwear)?
If something doesn't work, now is the time to find out .... ☐

Ensured your partner and all bridesmaids have done the same? .... ☐

Gently probed groom and his best man about speech content? You don't want
any horrid surprises.. ☐

If the ceremony is at church and you are not regular worshippers, have you been
to a service to take in the atmosphere? .... ☐

TOP TIP

Your mind will race during the week leading up to the wedding but it is important to sleep well. Sprinkle lavender oil on your pillow if necessary and make a conscious effort to go to bed early with something relaxing to read. Not your wedding's cuttings book or your guest list.

One week and counting ☑

Confirmed final numbers with caterers (including vegetarian meals and special dietary requirements)? . . . . ☐

Contacted key players the night before the rehearsal to remind them of the time? . . ☐

Sent final seating plan to the venue? (You have to draw the line somewhere and if people still haven't replied they are not very good friends!) . . . . ☐

Sent place names to the venue? Ensure all names are correctly spelled and easy to copy out if the place names are being written out by the venue staff.. . . . . ☐

Run through where everyone will be on the big day? Compare it to where they should be. Anyone been overlooked when you were working out the transport and lifts? . . . . ☐

Entrusted your handbag, make-up bag and overnight bag to someone? Do it now, not on the day. People don't mind being responsible for things if they have enough warning. . . . . ☐

Had a good massage or an aromatherapy session?. . . . . ☐

The day before... ☑

Had a romantic lunch with your fiancé (discussing non-wedding issues if possible)? ☐

Checked the weather forecast? Act accordingly. Hoping it won't rain may not be enough. If paths to the church/venue are likely to be muddy, can someone prepare a temporary walkway?. . . . . ☐

Panicked? No, not really! If you haven't done it by now, it's a bit late. If you've dipped into this guide and followed these checklists, it is unlikely you will have forgotten anything really serious. As they say Stateside – have a nice day!

TOP TIP

Make your loved one the first person you call on the morning of the wedding and don't forget to tell him you love him. The next chance you get to speak privately will be after you are married!

▶ # Budget planner

No wedding is likely to need everything listed here. However, it is better to consider all possibilities and then write 'not applicable' than to overlook something.

Wedding costs

	Estimate	Cost/quote
Engagement ring		
Wedding rings		
Newspaper announcements		
Engagement photos		
Church fees/licence		
Extras (choir, bells)		
Copyright fees (if extra)		
Registrar/legal fees		
Wedding insurance		
Venue hire (ceremony)		
Venue hire (reception)		
Marquee hire		
Marquee equipment hire		
Catering – food		
Catering – staff (if extra)		
Drinks reception		
Canapes		
Drinks with the meal		
Evening bar		
Late night snacks/coffees		
Wedding cake		
Extras (ice sculptures)		
Wedding cars		
Transport for guests		
Photography (including prints)		
Videographer		
Flowers for ceremony		
Flowers for reception		

	Deposit	Balance	Who pays?	☑
				☐
				☐
				☐
				☐
				☐
				☐
				☐
				☐
				☐
				☐
				☐
				☐
				☐
				☐
				☐
				☐
				☐
				☐
				☐
				☐
				☐
				☐
				☐
				☐
				☐
				☐
				☐

Wedding costs... (continued)

	Estimate	Cost/quote	
Bouquets and buttonholes			
Flowers as a gift/thank-you			
Petals as confetti			
Other thank-you gifts			
Decorations (candles, balloons)			
Musicians for the ceremony			
Musicians for the reception			
Entertainers (magicians, clowns)			
Master of ceremonies			
Band or DJ			
Children's crèche			
Favours for the table			
Single-use cameras			
Stationery and postage			
First night's hotel			
Honeymoon			
Spending money			
Transport to airport			
Bride's dress			
Lingerie			
Shoes			
Veil or headdress			
Hair and make-up			
Earrings or other jewellery			
Groom's outfit			
Groom's accessories			
Bridesmaids' dresses			
Bridesmaids headdresses			
Page boys/flower girls outfits			
Cushions for rings			
Memories book/guest book			
Contributions to stag night			
Contributions to hen night			
Outfit cleaning bills			

	Deposit	Balance	Who pays?	
				☑
				☐
				☐
				☐
				☐
				☐
				☐
				☐
				☐
				☐
				☐
				☐
				☐
				☐
				☐
				☐
				☐
				☐
				☐
				☐
				☐
				☐
				☐
				☐
				☐
				☐
				☐
				☐
				☐
				☐
				☐

Ceremony contacts

Over the coming months there will be a lot of phone calls and a few face-to-face meetings as you prepare for your wedding and honeymoon. In haste, it is very easy to scribble numbers and addresses on slips of paper and shove them in a pocket or bag because you are in a hurry. It is equally easy to lose them and only realize half an hour before you're supposed to be somewhere important. Make life easy for yourself and record everyone's contact details here.

Church of England ☑

Parish address for ceremony . . . .
Vicar's name and telephone . . . .
Date of first meeting. . . . .
Parish of bride/groom (if different) . . . .
Vicar's name and telephone . . . .

Documentation
Birth certificates. . . . . ☐
Baptism certificate (if required) . . . . ☐
Decree absolute (if divorced) . . . . ☐
Death certificate (if widowed) . . . . ☐

Checklist
Banns organized (bride's parish)? . . . . ☐
Banns organized (groom's parish, if different)? . . . . ☐
Wedding booked? . . . . ☐

TOP TIP

If you are asked to produce official certificates (Birth, Baptism, Decree Absolute, Death), take a photocopy before you remove them from their usual place of safe-keeping and put them in your bag/car, etc. If they should get mislaid, at least you will have the date and place of issue details.

Civil wedding ☑

Superintendent Registrar for district of proposed wedding

Name . . . .

Telephone . . . .

E-mail address . . . .

Appointment date . . . .

Superintendent Registrar in district where bride lives (if different)

Name. . . . .

Telephone . . . .

E-mail address . . . .

Appointment date . . . .

Superintendent Registrar in district where groom lives (if different)

Name. . . . .

Telephone . . . .

E-mail address . . . .

Appointment date . . . .

Documentation

Birth certificates. . . . . ☐

Decree absolute (if divorced) . . . . ☐

Death certificate (if widowed). . . . . ☐

Checklist

Fee for entry into marriage notice book paid? . . . . ☐

Marriage certificate organized? . . . . ☐

Date to collect certificate confirmed?. . . . . ☐

Registrar booked? . . . . ☐

TOP TIP

If you have queries about anything, however minor, don't hesitate to pick up the phone and ask your official/minister/registrar. You are not being a nuisance, you are being efficient and showing an interest. It is their job to reassure and inform you and, usually, they are happy to do it.

Other religious ceremonies ☑

Superintendent Registrar in district where bride lives

Name. . . . .

Telephone . . . .

E-mail address . . . .

Appointment date . . . .

Superintendent Registrar in district where groom lives (if different)

Name. . . . .

Telephone . . . .

E-mail address . . . .

Appointment date . . . .

Documentation

Birth certificates. . . . . □

Decree absolute (if divorced) . . . . □

Death certificate (if widowed) . . . . □

Checklist

Fee for entry into marriage notice book paid? . . . . □

Marriage certificate organized? . . . . □

Date to collect certificate confirmed? . . . . □

Place of worship for ceremony . . . .

Minister's name . . . .

Minister's telephone number . . . .

Date of first meeting. . . . .

Documentation

Birth certificates. . . . . □

Decree absolute (if divorced) . . . . □

Death certificate (if widowed) . . . . □

Checklist

Banns organized (if necessary)? . . . . □

Wedding booked? . . . . □